The Master's Book of Pool and Billiards

by Joe Stone

Foreword by Willie Mosconi

Crown Publishers, Inc., New York

© 1979 by Crown Publishers, Inc.

All rights reserved. No part of this book may be reproduced or utilized in any form or by any means, electronic or mechanical, including photocopying, recording, or by any information storage and retrieval system, without permission in writing from the publisher. Inquiries should be addressed to Crown Publishers, Inc., One Park Avenue, New York, N.Y. 10016.

Printed in the United States of America

Published simultaneously in Canada by General Publishing Company Limited

Library of Congress Cataloging in Publication Data

Stone, Joe.
  The master's book of pool and billiards.

  Includes index.
  1. Pool (Game) 2. Billiards. I. Title.
GV891.S83 1978   794.7'3   78-10362
ISBN 0-517-53568-8
ISBN 0-517-53418-5 pbk.

Contents

Foreword by Willie Mosconi	4
Preface	5
Introduction	6
Equipment	8
Fundamentals	9
Pool	14
Pool Diagrams	18
Billiards	44
Billiard Diagrams	45
Review Notes	91
Glossary	92
Index	95

Foreword

The author of this book, Joe Stone, has been a friend of mine for about thirty-five years. In 1941, I was playing in a Three-Cushion Caroms Tournament in New York City and not doing too well. It occurred to me that maybe my friend Joe Stone (who even then was known as an authority on this game) could give me a few pointers to help my game. He did, and in two hours I learned enough to win my next three games from top opponents.

Joe Stone began teaching professionally in 1963, and in 1966, while I was giving an exhibition in New York City, I made the statement to an audience of 300 people that I had found that Joe Stone is the best billiards teacher in the world, both for Three-Cushion Caroms and Pocket Billiards.

From that time until now, my liking for Joe Stone as a teacher and as a man has steadily increased. I call him a real champion.

Willie Mosconi

Preface

For many years I have loved the game of billiards, and have always felt that there has never been enough publicity of the right kind to make the game attractive to the general public. Also, no real effort has been made to teach the various games of billiards.

I have read nearly all the published books on these games, but have not found any that teaches the two most popular games, Pocket Billiards and Three-Cushion Caroms, in the way I would like them to be taught.

Maybe I'm a cranky old curmudgeon, or maybe I expect too much, but I have found too many faults in the books I've read. Some are too academic, some much too personal. Diagrams are often inaccurate and generally more confusing than enlightening. Some books cover one game well, some others, but none covers both games well enough. There are other faults, but that's plenty. They just don't do the job right. I know this book will do it better.

Beginners may have a little trouble mastering the fundamentals, but they must work hard on them as they will give their game the correct foundation. When they have developed correct stance, stroke, bridge, and body balance, they will enjoy these games immensely even while they continue to learn.

Good players will learn many new shots, and get some valuable tips about billiards in general, which will improve their game and also give more confidence. My experience as a teacher has proved this many times.

Professionals will also strengthen their knowledge of billiards. This book may also serve to correct minor faults that may have crept into their game, possibly even show them a few shots that they do not use often enough. For example, there are very few players who know and utilize the full value of a good draw stroke.

Joe Stone

Introduction

Pool and billiards are fascinating, enjoyable, and throughly rewarding games. They have a definite value as a mild exercise and they can be played by people of all ages. In many ways, they are demanding games, but, after the fundamentals are mastered to a certain extent, it is not at all difficult to attain a very satisfactory degree of proficiency.

The requirements for playing well are practically the same as in most other sports: good eyesight (not entirely essential), body balance, good hands, and good coordination are the main ones, and the knowledge and experience to pick the right shot—that is, the shot that is most likely to score and lead to successive scoring.

To become a champion or even a near champion you need everything mentioned above, plus a willingness to study, realizing that there are myriad angles and possibilities in the various games of billiards.

You also need a strong desire to win, a natural instinct for the game, the ability to concentrate, to keep on learning, and, above all, the necessary poise to accept bad breaks without losing your stroke or your composure.

Many varied and fanciful accounts have been written about the origin of the game of billiards. References are found in the Greek philosophers, even before Caesar, and a French writer named Bonhomme wrote in 1885 that, had Nero played billiards instead of fiddling, all subsequent history might have been changed.

England, France, Italy, Spain, and China are all mentioned as inventing billiards, but no definite origin has been established.

A great French player, Maurice Vignaux, whom Willie Hoppe defeated in 1906 for the World's Balk-Line Championship, when questioned as to the origin of billiards disclaimed any knowledge about it, but did say that Shakespeare, Ben Jonson, and Lord Byron mentioned billiards several times in their writings.

King Louis XIV was reputed to be an ardent devotee of billiards, as was also Mary Queen of Scots.

England was probably not the birthplace of billiards, but it seems that the game was played there more than anywhere else.

It was the Spaniards who brought billiards to St. Augustine, Florida, in 1565. The game grew gradually in the Western Hemisphere until it became associated with America more than with any other country.

Many famous men, such as George Washington, Thomas Jefferson, Alexander Hamilton, the Marquis de Lafayette, Abraham Lincoln, and Theodore Roosevelt, have also liked the ivory game.

In my own time I have met many famous people who liked pool and billiards, notable among whom was Mark Twain, whom I saw play at Slosson's Billiard Room, 22nd Street and Broadway, New York, in 1902. He was then sixty-nine years old. Among the others were Irwin Cobb, O. Henry, Jack London, and Damon Runyon.

As to pool, it seems to be just an offshoot of billiards, and did not reach important status until 1859, when a match game was played between Michael Phelan of New York City and John Secreiter of Detroit, Michigan. Mr. Phelan won the match by the score of 2000 to 1904.

Since that time, in spite of the fact that pool has had bad publicity rather than good, the game has grown greatly in popularity—so much so that I believe over 30 million people in the United States are playing some form of billiards now, and thousands of tables are being installed in private homes.

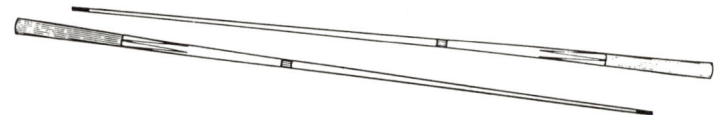

Equipment

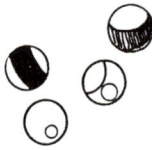

For pocket billiards the size of the table for championship matches or tournament play is 4½ feet wide by 9 feet long. This is called the standard size. Tables may be smaller or larger, but should always be twice as long as they are wide. The width of the pockets may range from 4¾ inches to 5½ inches. The balls used should be 2¼ inches in diameter, numbered from 1 to 15.

Cues generally run from 15 to 23 ounces in weight, but 18, 19, and 20 are used most often. The length should be 55 inches to 58 inches, and the tip from 12 to 13½ millimeters in diameter. The cue should be balanced correctly so that it feels good to you.

For Three-Cushion Caroms, the table size is 5 feet by 10 feet. This is the championship or standard size. Some tables are made 4½ feet by 9 feet and this does not change the game to any great extent, but if any smaller tables were to be used, the game would probably be less attractive.

The balls used for billiards should be 2 25/64 inches in diameter. This was the standard size when ivory balls were used. At present plastic or synthetic ivory is used and many tournaments are played in which the rules call for the balls to be 2 27/64 inches in diameter. The difference, it seems to me, is not important.

Fundamentals

Do not rush your study of fundamentals. They are the foundation of your game and to know them solidly will add to your enjoyment of all forms of billiards. You must know stance, grip, bridge, stroke, follow-through, and draw. You must know how to cue the shooting ball (cue ball), how to hit the object ball, and how to chalk up. You must also study the use of English and position play. Now, to take up these items step by step.

Stance

Stance is your position at the table. Of course no two people will stand or play exactly alike. The rules and methods given here are the orthodox ones, but a player must learn his or her own best style and the important word throughout your learning is **adjustment,** as you will find out. However, my advice is to try to stay as near as you can to the orthodox method. You must also learn to be perfectly relaxed so that you can play without too much strain or effort.

Stand at the table, facing it in the direction of your shot. In actual play your distance from the table will vary depending on the position of the cue ball, but for now stand about 12 inches from the table. Your feet should be about 6 to 8 inches apart, with your right foot in line with the shot. Turn both feet slightly to the right and move your right foot back and bend forward. Your weight should be evenly distributed on both legs, with your left knee somewhat more bent than your right. The cue is held about 4 inches from your body. The left arm is extended to form a bridge for the cue about 9 inches from the tip. Your head must always be over the cue in the line of aim. Your body may move forward very slightly as you hit the cue ball, beginning the correct follow-through.

Grip and Bridge

Select a cue that feels good to you. Champion Willie Mosconi says that the cue he uses is 57 inches long and weighs 19½ ounces. The tip is 13 millimeters in diameter. My experience over the years tells me that these specifications are practically perfect for the average-sized man. For especially short or tall people, or for women, a slight change is advised.

Grip: First find the balance point of the cue. I find the best balance point 16½ to 17 inches from the butt. Grip the cue so that the right thumb is about 4 inches below the balance point. Grip the cue slightly so that the thumb and three fingers actually touch the cue. Too tight a grip takes away your feel and may also deaden the action of the cue ball.

The Bridge: This refers to how you hold the forward part of the cue in your left hand. There are many different bridges, but the most common one is created by making a fist with your left hand and opening up the thumb and index finger to form a V. Lay shaft on the thumb and wrap the index finger over the cue shaft. Close the thumb over index finger. Now extend the other fingers in a wide, flat web, with fingertips on the cloth. You may rest the heel of your hand on the table, but if you have a strong wrist and strong fingers this is not necessary. Find your own way.

The bridge hand should be very firm and the shaft of the cue should be held so that you feel it wrinkling your thumb.

Aiming and Hitting the Object Ball

There has always been discussion as to what the player should look at before hitting the cue ball—the object ball or the cue ball. I simply cannot advise the reader on this point. Only practice will teach you the best way.

Before shooting, look at the line as though you were going to shoot the object ball into the pocket. That gives you the correct target. Cover that spot with the center of the cue ball.

The Stroke and Follow-Through

Developing a good stroke depends mainly on gripping the cue correctly—lightly but firmly—and on having a good bridge.

Your position at the table must be balanced and relaxed, and your head should be over the cue in the line of aim. If all this is correct, the cue will swing gracefully. As you stroke swinging back and forth, the shoulder moves very slightly; the elbow and the wrist supply the necessary force. You must have rhythm in your stroke.

The follow-through is difficult to teach; it will come to you either naturally or by steady practice. However, avoid pushing with your cue after you stroke: the cue tip, before you draw it back should be about two inches beyond the spot where your cue tip was while you made your preliminary strokes. Don't lift your cue quickly after hitting the cue ball. The stroke should be a smooth, easy motion of the wrist and elbow.

The Draw Stroke and the Follow Stroke

To control the position of the cue ball on the table after shooting, the most important factor is to be able to draw or follow. On the draw stroke, the cue ball rolls back toward the shooter after contact with the object ball. On the follow stroke, the cue ball rolls along after the object ball.

The draw is done by striking the cue ball below center, using a low bridge and getting a sharp wrist snap into the stroke.

Follow is achieved by a smooth even stroke, an orthodox bridge, and hitting the cue ball about one cue tip diameter above its center.

The Use of English

Learning to use English—that is, putting spin on the cue ball—is difficult at first but becomes fairly easy after practice.

To make it short, when you hit to the right of the center of the cue ball, it will curve to the right. Hitting to the left of center makes the ball curve to the left.

When you put English on the cue ball and direct it toward the object ball, the effect is to send that object ball in an opposite direction to the way you have applied the English. Right English on the cue ball sends the object ball to the left, and vice versa.

The amount of deflection or throw is approximately 6 inches in 36 inches.

Five Ways to Hit the Cue Ball

First of all, correct chalking up is essential. Brush the cue tip with several light but sure strokes, making certain a thin, even coating is spread on the tip. Chalk up often and avoid using a piece of chalk with a deep hole.

A) If you hit the cue ball dead center with medium force and just a slight snap of the wrist, you will create what is called a stop shot; that is, the cue ball stops after having hit the object ball.

B) In a follow shot, hit the cue ball with slightly less force one cue-tip diameter above center. The cue ball will then follow the object ball.

C) In the draw shot, the cue ball is struck one cue-tip diameter or slightly more below center. The cue ball will then draw away from the object ball after hitting it, moving backward toward the shooters.

D and E) By using left-hand or right-hand English—that is, by hitting the cue ball left or right of center—both cue ball and object ball can be made to curve left or right.

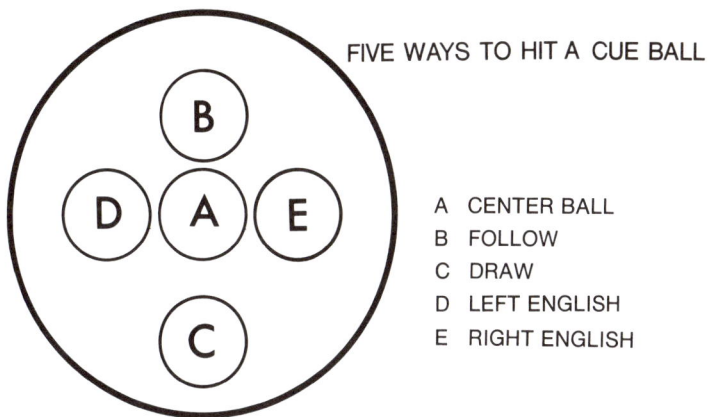

Position Play

Playing for position is really the name of the game in pocket billiards. It means handling the cue ball in such a way as to be in the best position to continue pocketing balls. To do this well means knowing just how to hit the cue ball (correct speed and English), and how to carry in one's mind the layout of the various balls. You must also understand carom points. The carom point is the spot on the first cushion struck by the shooting ball. If the center ball is used, a perfect isosceles triangle is formed, from the object ball to the carom point to the point where the cue ball strikes the next cushion.

Seeing this triangle perfectly is the basis for position play in pool, and for scoring correctly at Three Cushions.

What to Play

The main pocket billiard games are the 14–1 Straight Pool game, Rotation, Eight Ball, Nine Ball, and One Pocket.

The main billiard or carom games are Straight Billiards, Balk-Line Billiards, Red Ball, and Three-Cushion Caroms.

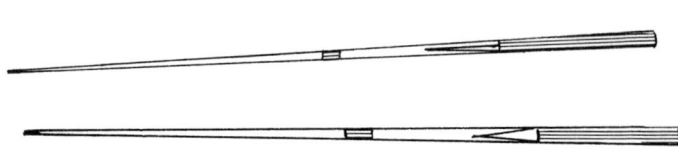

Pool

Straight Pool

The fifteen object balls are racked in a pyramid at the foot spot and the player has the cue ball in hand.

The minimum requirements of the opening break are that the player drive the cue ball and at least two object balls to the cushion. This is called an opening safety shot.

The other player then tries to pocket a ball or "play safe," and the game proceeds with the players taking turns at the table pocketing one ball after another without regard to numbers until one player misses. Only fourteen balls are pocketed, leaving one ball on the table for the next break shot. The fourteen balls are racked up and the player continues shooting until he or she misses.

On all shots after the opening, the player must call the ball he tries to pocket. If he fails, he loses his turn at the table, but is not otherwise penalized. If a player calls a ball, and makes it in his pocket, any other balls sunk on that shot are his. If he misses his called ball, other pocketed balls are respotted.

Play continues until fourteen balls are pocketed. The fifteenth and last object ball is saved for the next frame. When playable it is called the break shot. Players, of course, try to have as easy a break shot as possible and good position. Playing to get this shot is the real science of the game of pocket billiards.

Usually one point is forfeited if the player scratches, allowing the cue ball to go into a pocket. Failure to drive the cue ball or object ball to a cushion, either when trying for a shot or when playing safe, is another penalty, as is forcing the cue ball off the table. Other penalties are for interfering with the cue ball after the stroke, stroking when the cue ball is in motion, and failing to have one foot on the floor when shooting.

There are many house rules, and unexpected situations will arise. In all games where there is a referee, his decision is final. Where there is no referee, the house or manager becomes the referee.

Rotation

This is played with fifteen balls numbered from 1 to 15, totaling 120. The player who scores 61 points or more wins the game. Rotation, like Eight Ball, is a game that can be played by individuals or teams.

The balls are racked at the foot with the #1 ball at the top of the triangle, the #2 ball in the left corner, the #3 ball in the right corner, and the #15 ball in the center. The object of the game is to pocket the balls in numerical order. The count is also the numerical point value of the pocketed balls (#5 ball—5 points; #9 ball—9 points, etc.).

On every shot the player must strike the cue ball so that it makes contact with the proper object ball (the lowest numbered ball on the table).

If the cue ball fails to strike the proper object ball, the player does not get credit for any balls pocketed. Such balls must be spotted, removed from the pockets, and placed on the table again.

Eight Ball

In Eight Ball the fifteen balls are racked at the foot spot with the #8 ball in the center of the triangle. The balls are so divided that one player must pocket balls

#1 to #7 (the solid-colored balls) and the other player must pocket #9 to #15 (the striped balls). The players are not assigned their grouping until the first ball is pocketed, then the player who has pocketed the first ball announces his choice.

The object of the game is for the player to pocket the balls in his group in rotation, then the #8 ball. If he calls the #8 and makes it, he wins the game.

If a player accidentally pockets the #8 ball at any time during the game, he loses the game; or if a player scratches while shooting the #8 ball, he loses.

Each billiard room seems to have its own set of rules, but the above rules generally apply.

Nine Ball

This game is played with nine balls numbered from 1 to 9, and a cue ball. The balls are racked in a **diamond** on the foot spot in a definite order. The #1 ball is placed in the forward corner, the #2 ball in the left corner, the #3 ball in the rear corner, the #4 ball in the right corner, and the #9 ball in the center of the diamond. The winner of the game is the player who successfully pockets the #9 ball. The shooter has to sink the #1 ball first, and anything else pocketed is a bonus. The player continues until he or she misses. If the #9 ball drops in any pocket, he is immediately the winner. The shooter must strike the lowest numbered ball on the table (as in Rotation). No ball legally pocketed shall be placed back on table as a result of fouls. There are no penalties except loss of turn at the table.

The Shoot-Out Rule: When a player cannot hit the lowest numbered ball directly or thinks the shot is too difficult, he or she may roll the cue ball to another spot. The opponent then has the option of shooting or making the other player take the shot. If the opponent shoots and fails to hit the right ball, the player takes the cue ball in hand and may place it in any position desired to hit the lowest numbered object ball.

In this game of Nine Ball, house rules may vary, but seldom on important points.

One Pocket

This game is played with a cue ball and the regular fifteen balls. The fifteen balls are racked as in Straight Pool. Prior to the opening shot, the winner selects one pocket at the foot of the table as his or her pocket. The opponent uses the opposite pocket as the other foot of the table.

The opening player must try to make a ball in his pocket. A ball pocketed elsewhere is respotted. Usually the opening player plays for safety on the break, moving as many balls as possible near his pocket.

A player continues shooting until he fails to shoot a ball into his pocket. When he misses, the opponent, accepting the balls as he finds them, tries to pocket any object ball in his designated pocket. The first player to pocket eight balls is the winner.

The safety rules are the same as in Straight Pool, except that in the opening break the cue ball or object ball must be driven to a cushion.

If a player pockets a ball in his corner and at the same time puts a ball into his opponent's pocket, the opponent keeps that ball as if he had made it, but the player keeps shooting. Balls dropping in other pockets are respotted at the finish of the inning. If a player pockets a winning ball (the eighth) and at the same time pockets the winning ball of his opponent, he is the winner.

Various penalties exist, and compel the offending player to forfeit one ball plus others pocketed on the foul stroke. Fouls occur for the following reasons:

1. Failure on the opening break to drive two object balls to a cushion.
2. Scratching: Cue ball going into a pocket.
3. Forcing the cue ball off the table.
4. Failing to execute a legal safety.
5. Striking the cue ball twice on the same stroke.
6. Touching the cue ball with a hand or clothing (anything except tip of cue).

Pool Diagrams

Note on the Diagrams

In learning to play the various forms of pool and billiards, there is no substitute for practice. The techniques are not difficult to learn, but it takes years of experience to make the techniques work with regularity and precision. Since I cannot actually be with you at the pool table, I have made the basis of this book a series of pool table diagrams that will demonstrate both fundamental and advanced play. If you study these diagrams carefully, duplicate the setups on the actual table, and practice them, you will learn many subtleties of ball control as well as ways to perfect your aiming and stroking.

Both the pool and billiard tables in this book are, of course, drawn to scale, and show both the pockets and the aiming points along the cushions known as diamonds. The cue ball is always a white circle with a small arrow pointing in the direction of the shot. The object balls are black circles.

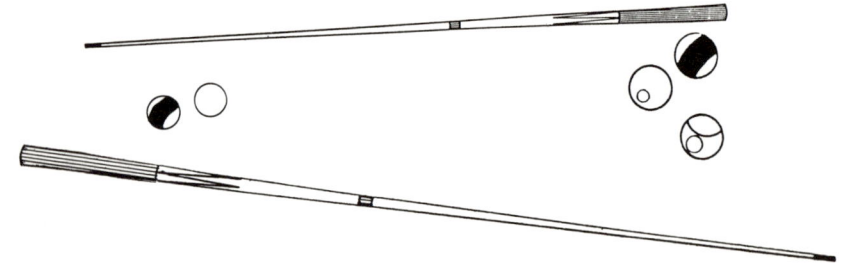

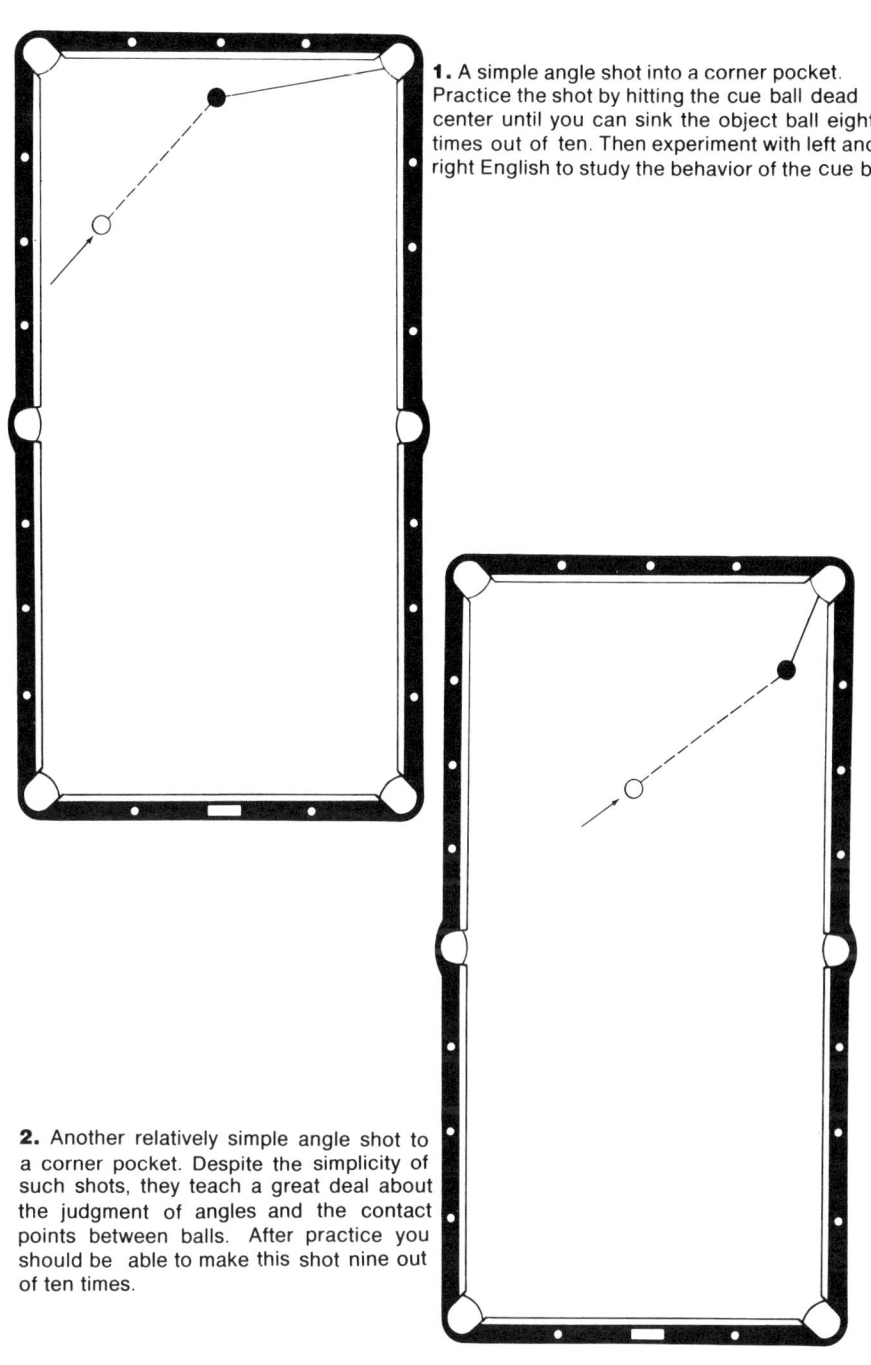

1. A simple angle shot into a corner pocket. Practice the shot by hitting the cue ball dead center until you can sink the object ball eight times out of ten. Then experiment with left and right English to study the behavior of the cue ball.

2. Another relatively simple angle shot to a corner pocket. Despite the simplicity of such shots, they teach a great deal about the judgment of angles and the contact points between balls. After practice you should be able to make this shot nine out of ten times.

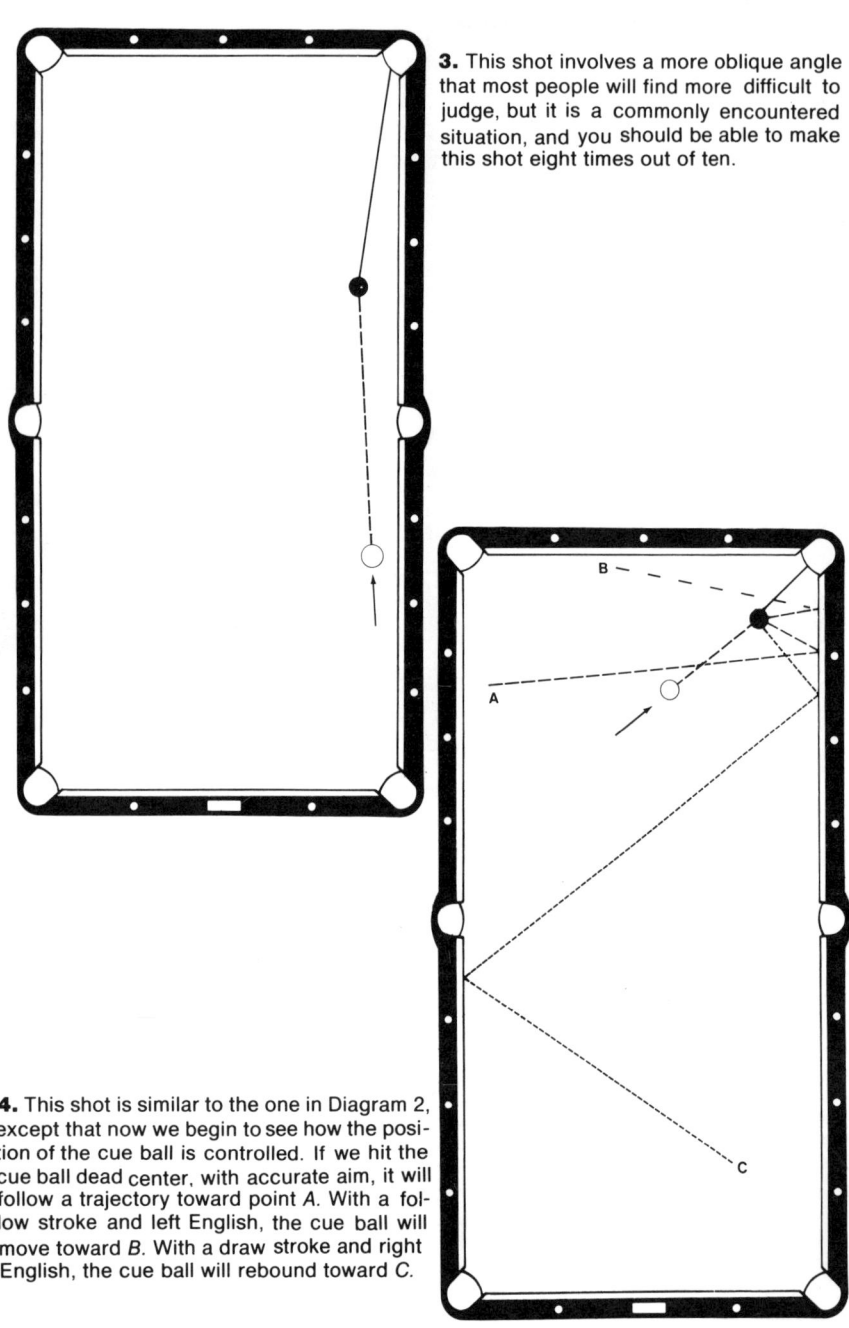

3. This shot involves a more oblique angle that most people will find more difficult to judge, but it is a commonly encountered situation, and you should be able to make this shot eight times out of ten.

4. This shot is similar to the one in Diagram 2, except that now we begin to see how the position of the cue ball is controlled. If we hit the cue ball dead center, with accurate aim, it will follow a trajectory toward point A. With a follow stroke and left English, the cue ball will move toward B. With a draw stroke and right English, the cue ball will rebound toward C.

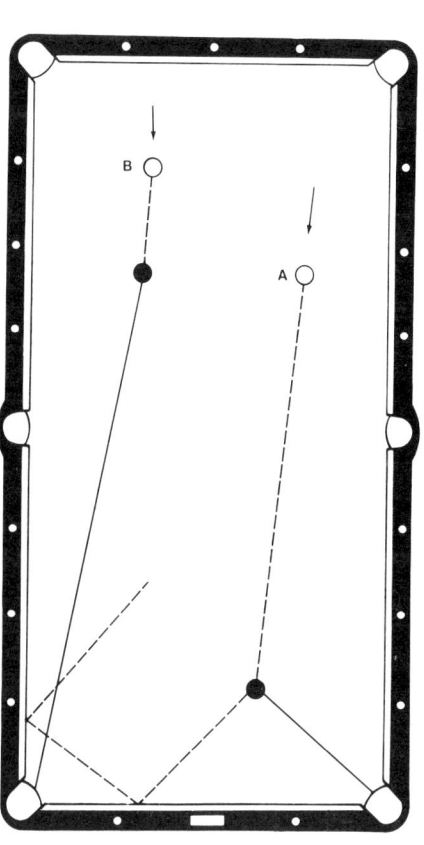

5. Here are two shots to practice often. They are similar, but require that the object balls be hit at different points.

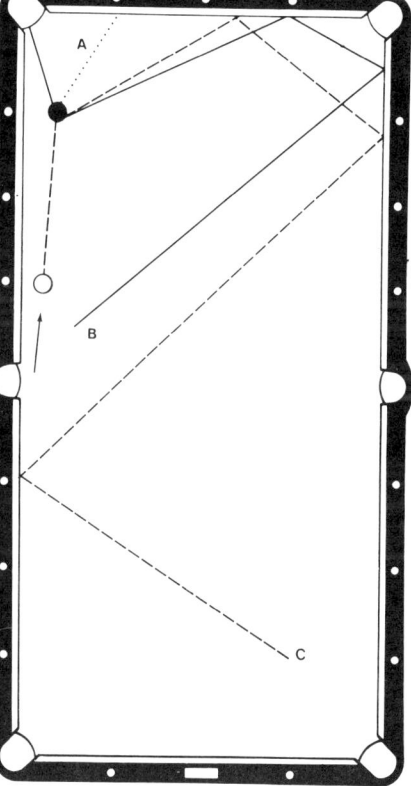

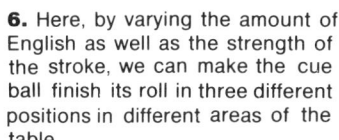

6. Here, by varying the amount of English as well as the strength of the stroke, we can make the cue ball finish its roll in three different positions in different areas of the table.

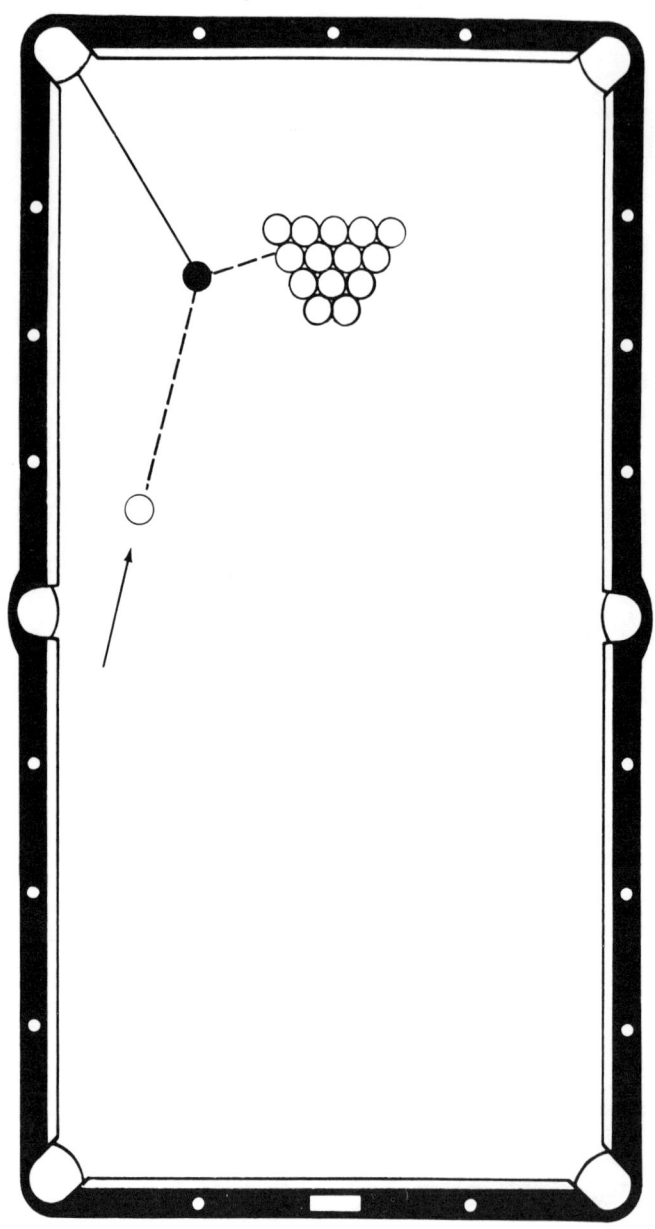

7. The most desired break. If you can maneuver into this position before the next rack, you are truly mastering position play.

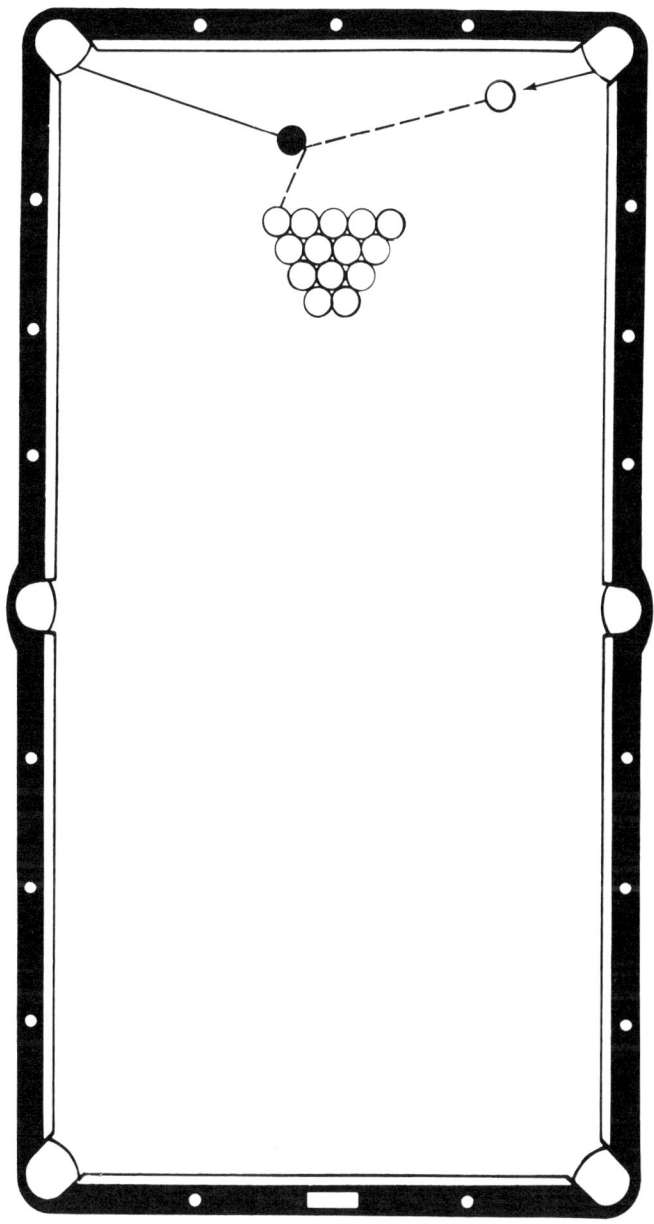

8. It is not uncommon for amateurs to find themselves behind a fairly solid rack of balls. In such cases mastery of this kind of shot is very useful.

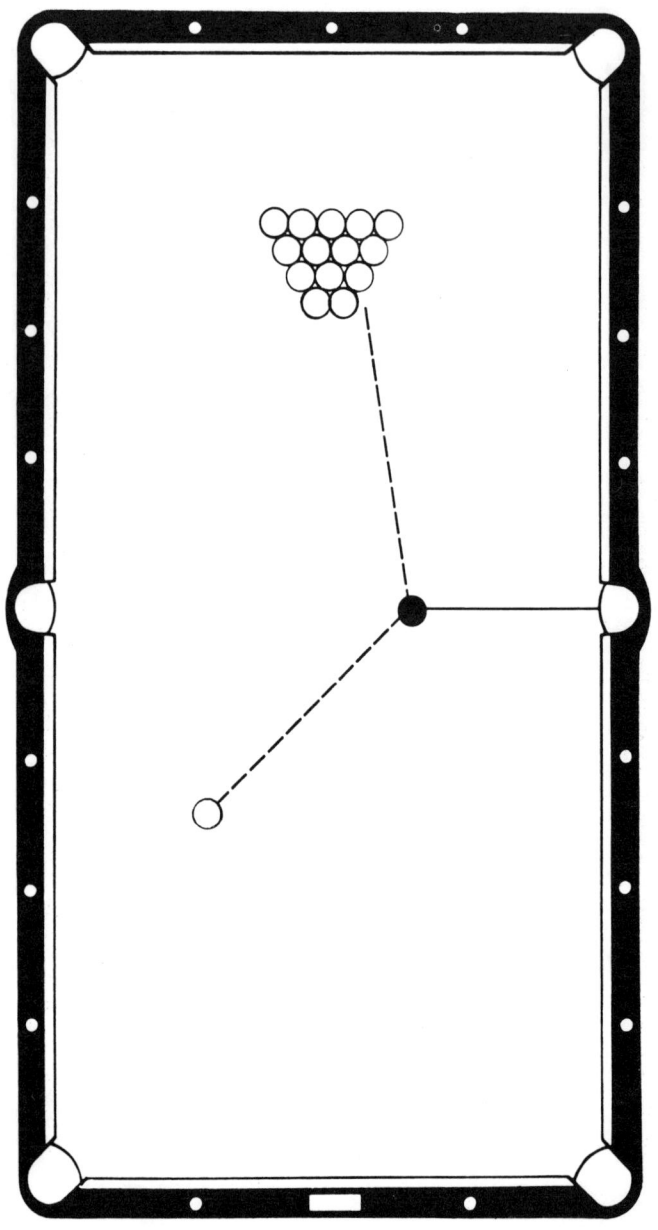

9. A direct break. The object ball is sunk in the side pocket and the rack is effectively smashed apart.

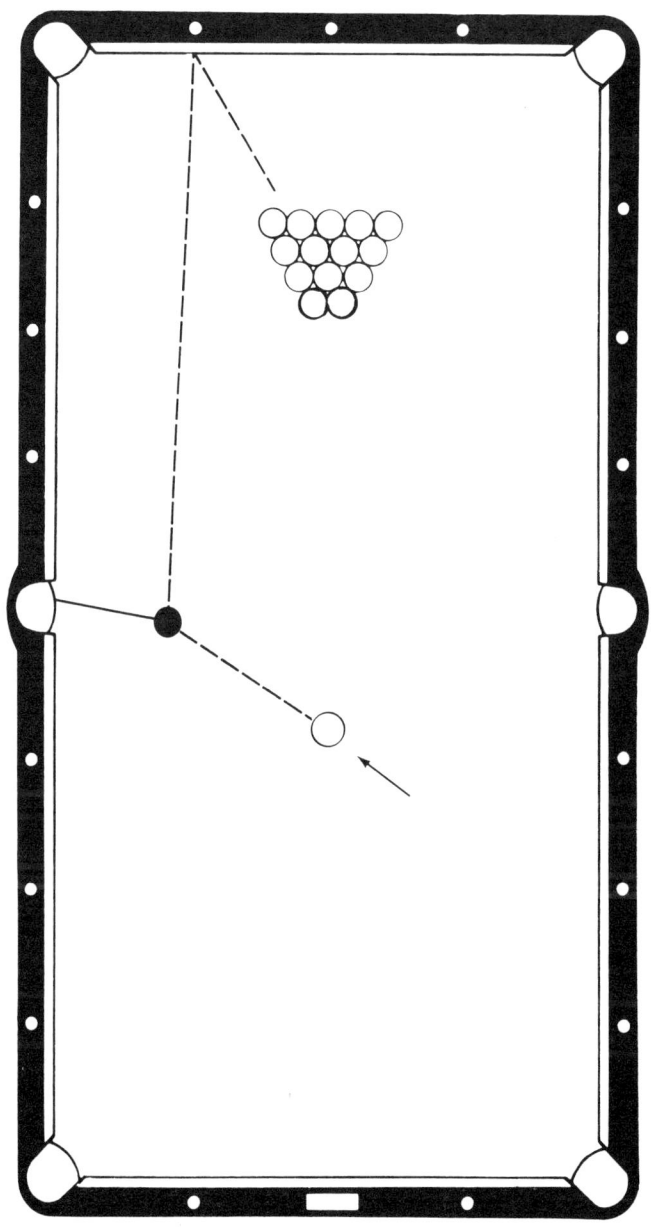

10. Only a small change in position can make a direct break impractical. This one-cushion break is another method of attacking the problem.

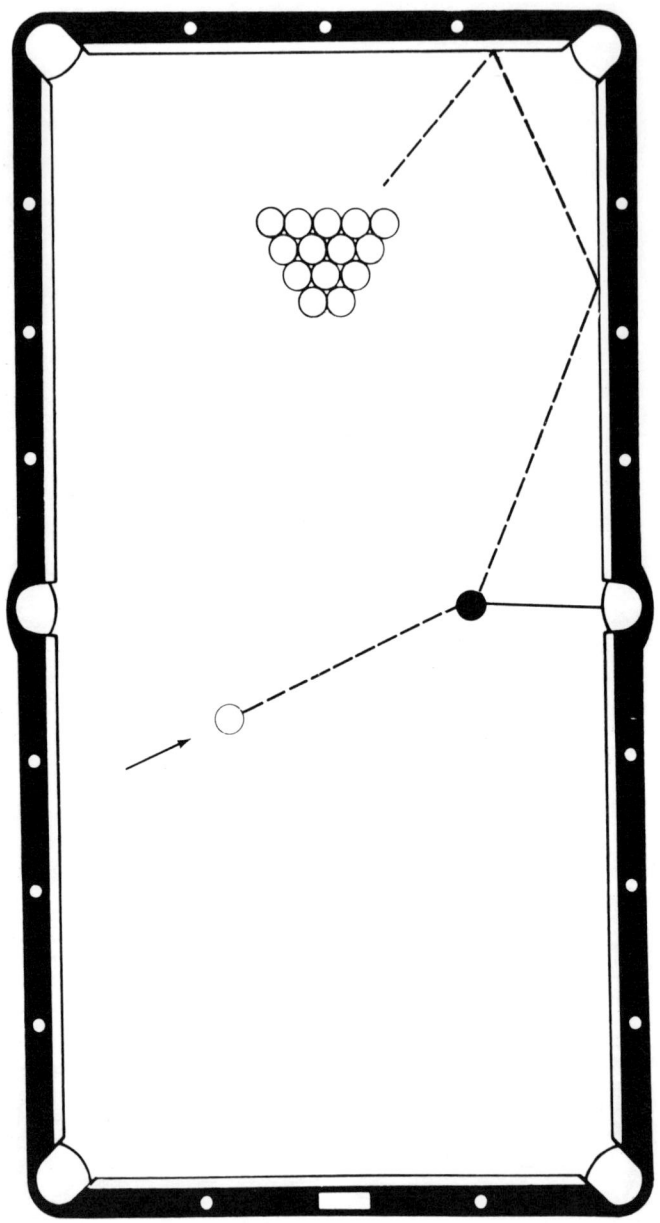

11. Still another method is this two-cushion break. Variations such as these demonstrate the importance of imagination in good pool playing.

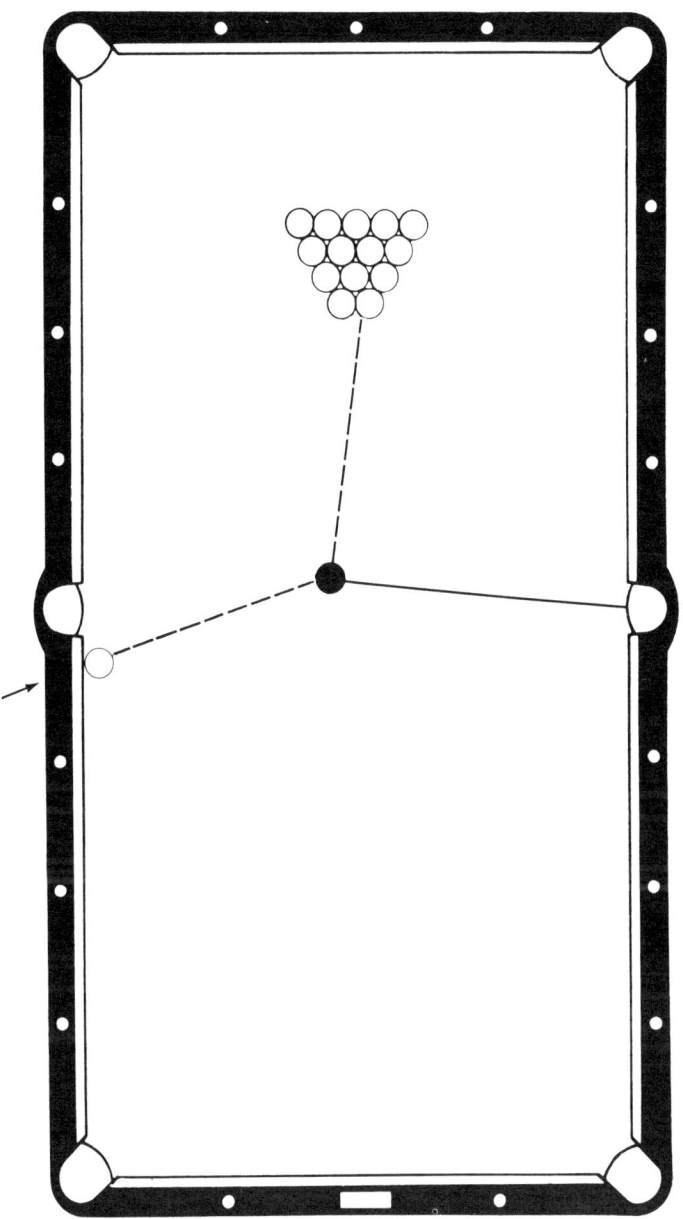

12. This is a very difficult break shot because the cue ball is frozen on the cushion, requiring a special bridge and great steadiness to make the shot come off.

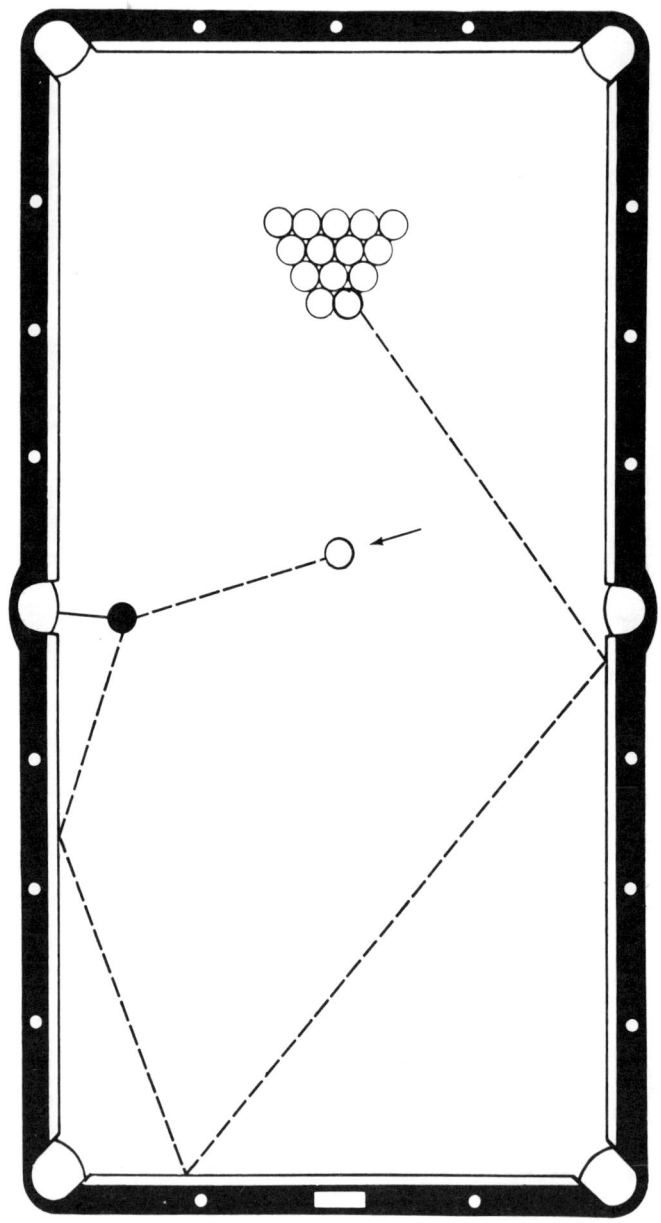

13. This three-cushion break is difficult and is not seen very often, though the table position leaves the shooter very little choice.

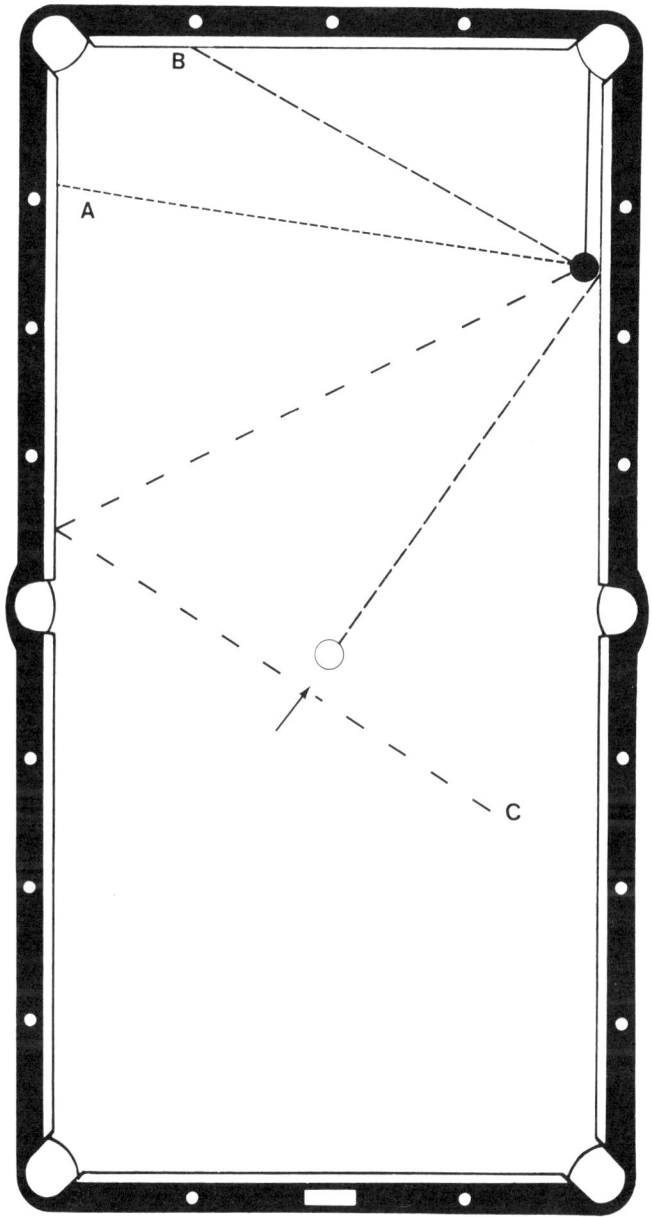

14. There are several possible solutions when an object ball is frozen against (in contact with) the cushion. Position A results from a dead-center hit. B is a follow stroke with left English, and C is a draw stroke with right English.

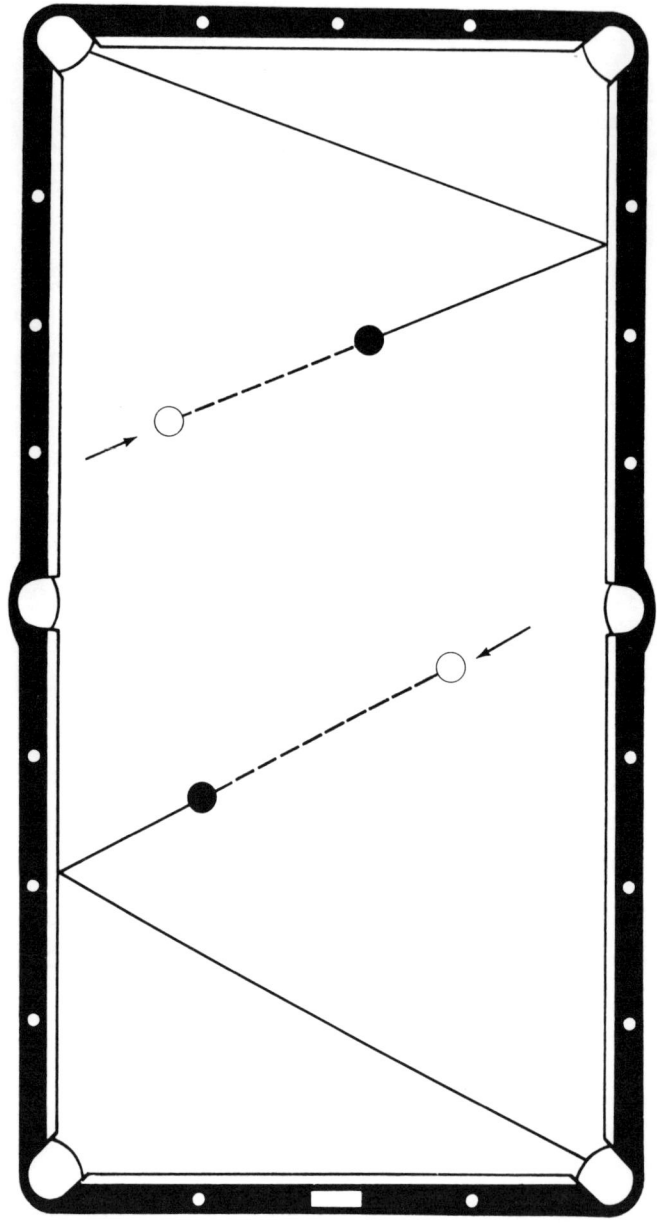

15. Two illustrations of the bank-shot triangle. Getting the angles right for this type of shot is not easy. Practice a lot, and pay particular attention to just where the object ball must strike the cushion. The diamonds on the rail will help you.

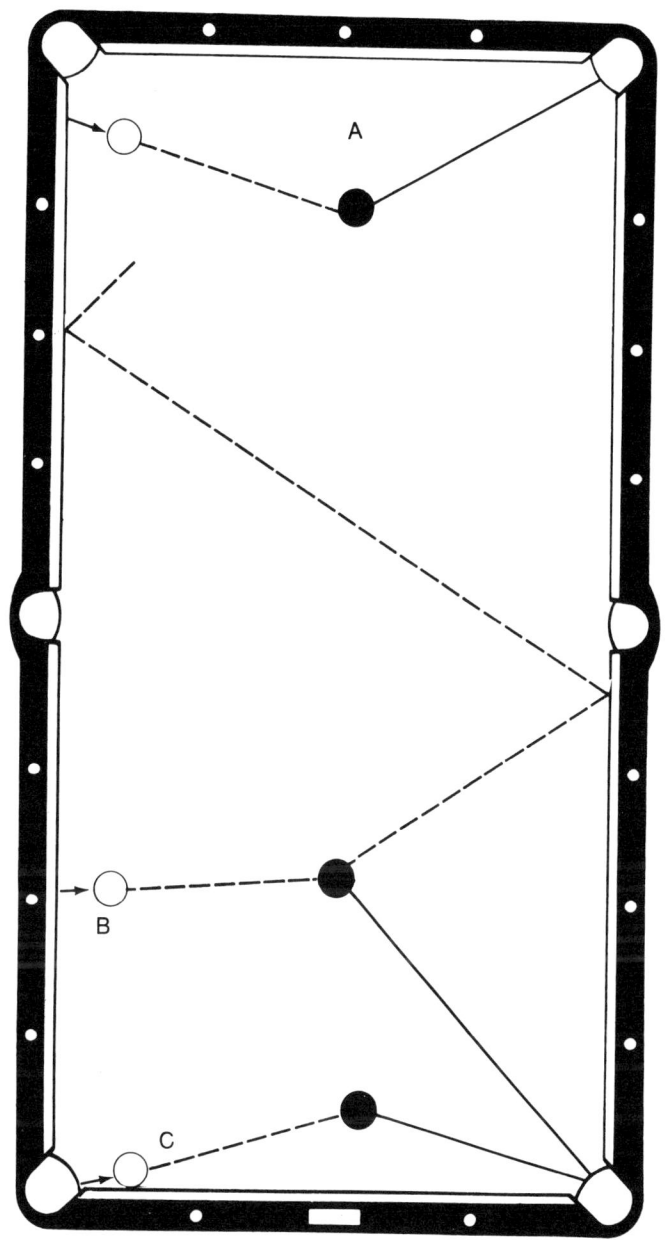

16. These three special shots occur quite frequently in pool and require that the player understand how to "cut" a ball. Basically, cutting means that the object ball is not hit dead center, but at an angle, so that its path can deviate from the straight-line roll of the cue ball that hits it. In practice this often means that the object ball is hit at a very fine angle, depending upon how much deviation is required. *A* is a difficult shot that can be made with a center ball stroke or left English. The object ball is just barely clipped to sink it. *B* is a similar shot. *C* is not so difficult because the angle of the cut is not so extreme.

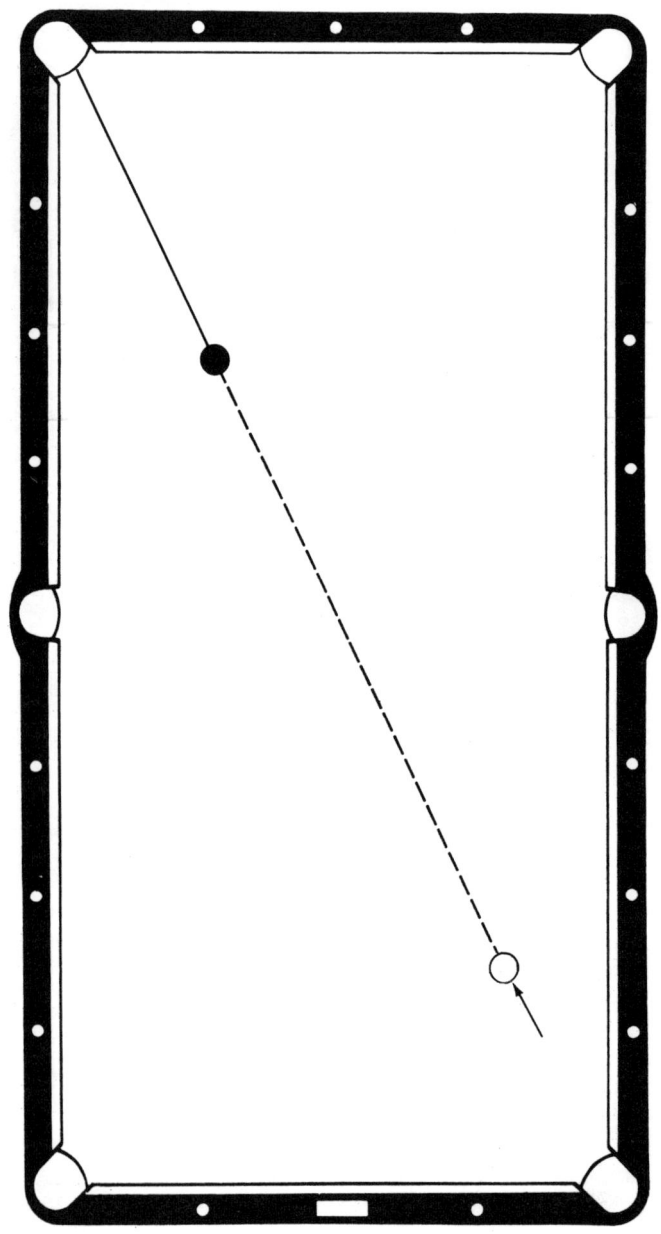

17. A long, straight cross-table shot to the opposite corner. The farther back the cue ball is from the object ball, the more difficult the shot. Practice this shot without English until you master it.

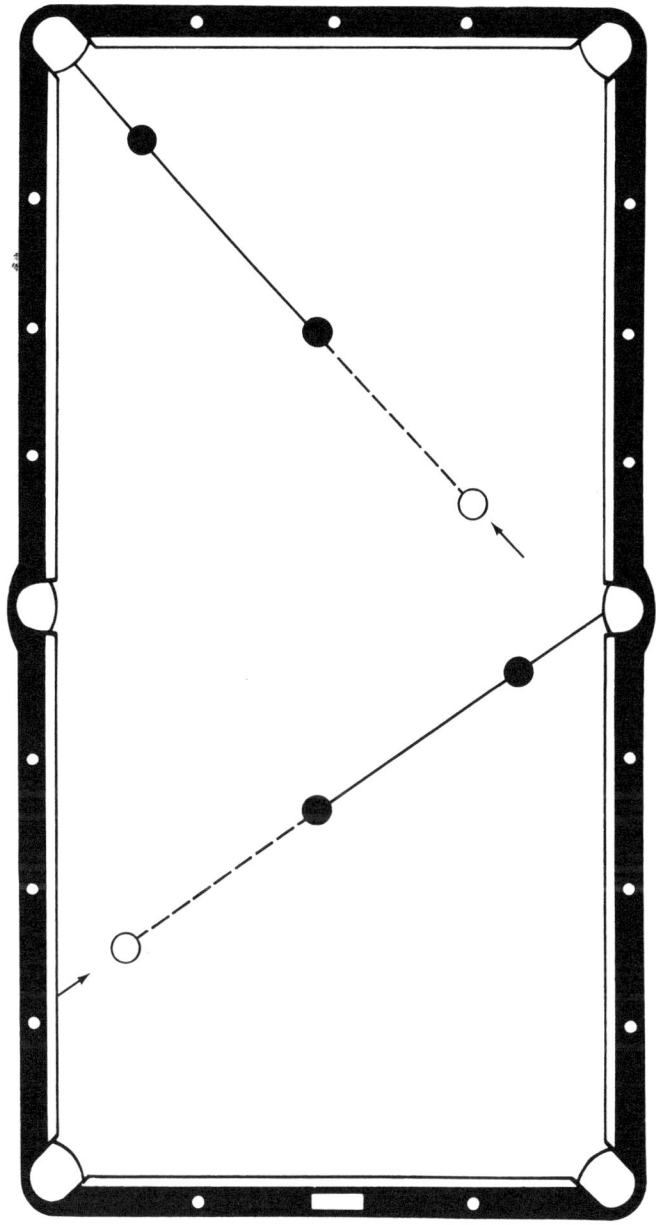

18. Two examples of a simple combination shot involving more than one object ball. These are straightforward shots that will test your ability to hit the cue ball dead center.

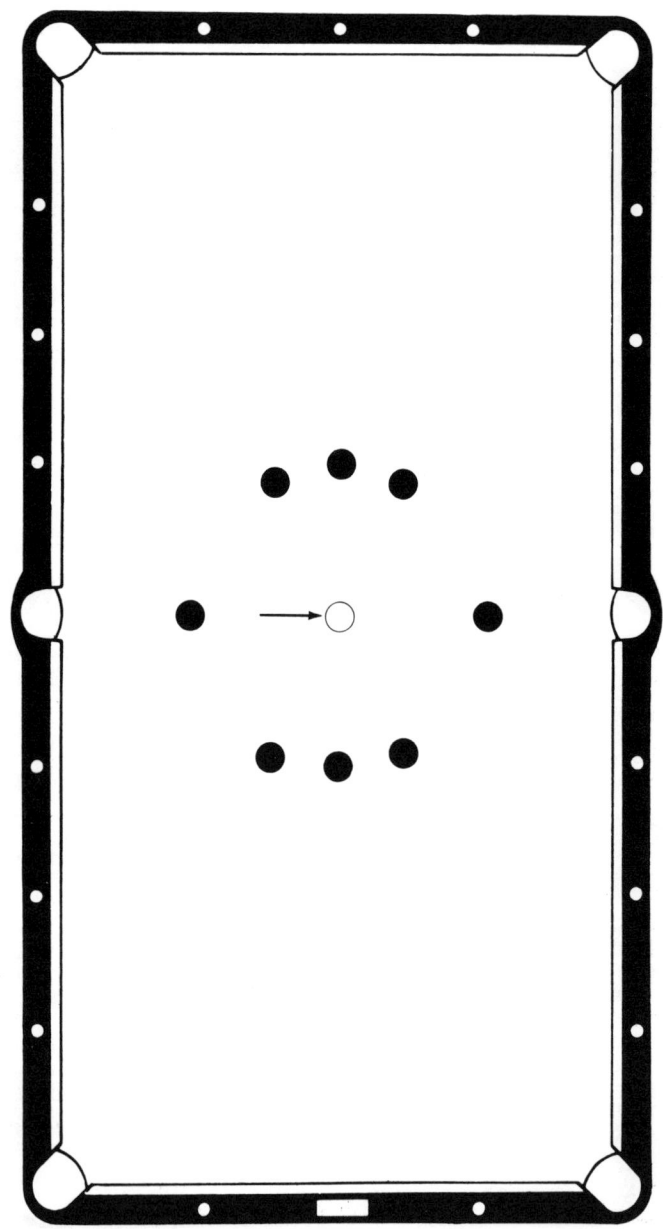

19. Here is an exercise that will really test you. When you can sink all eight balls you are well on your way to becoming a good player. The trick, of course, is to keep the cue ball in the center of the table, and this is accomplished with light, subtle draw strokes and some English.

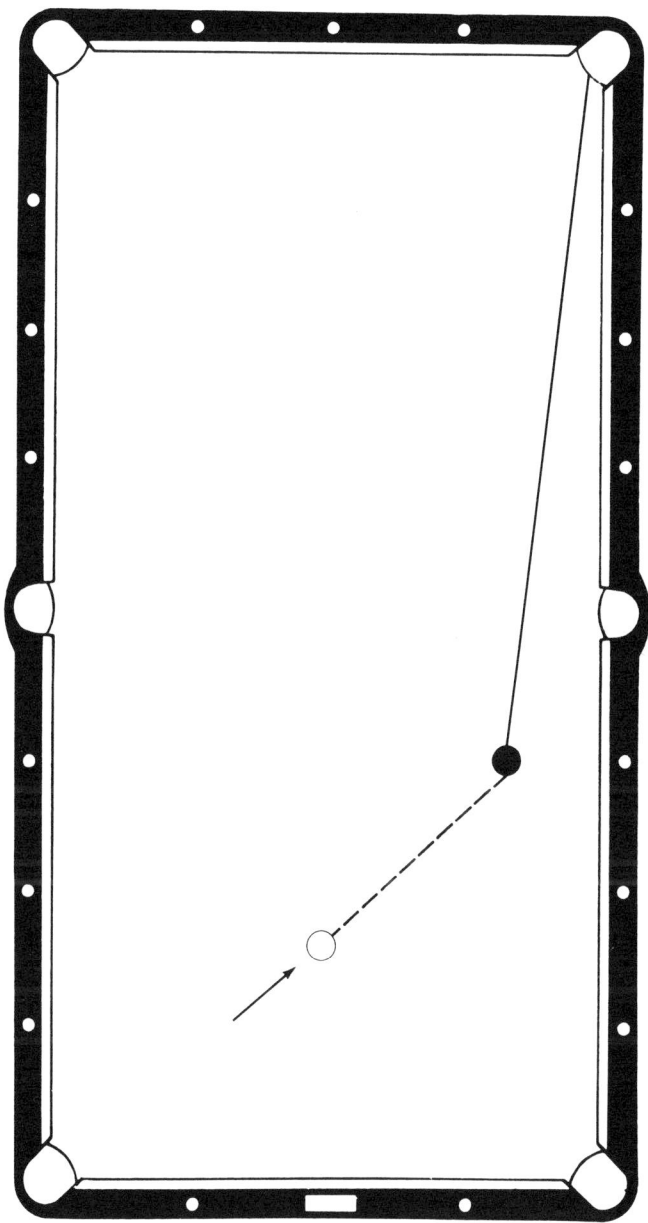

20. This is a long cut shot. A cut shot involves hitting the object ball somewhat off-center—that is, to one side of the center point as viewed from the cue ball. Anytime that the line from cue ball to object ball to pocket is not absolutely straight a cut shot will be used, because it is not the most forward point on the cue ball that must strike the object ball. Cut shots should be practiced frequently.

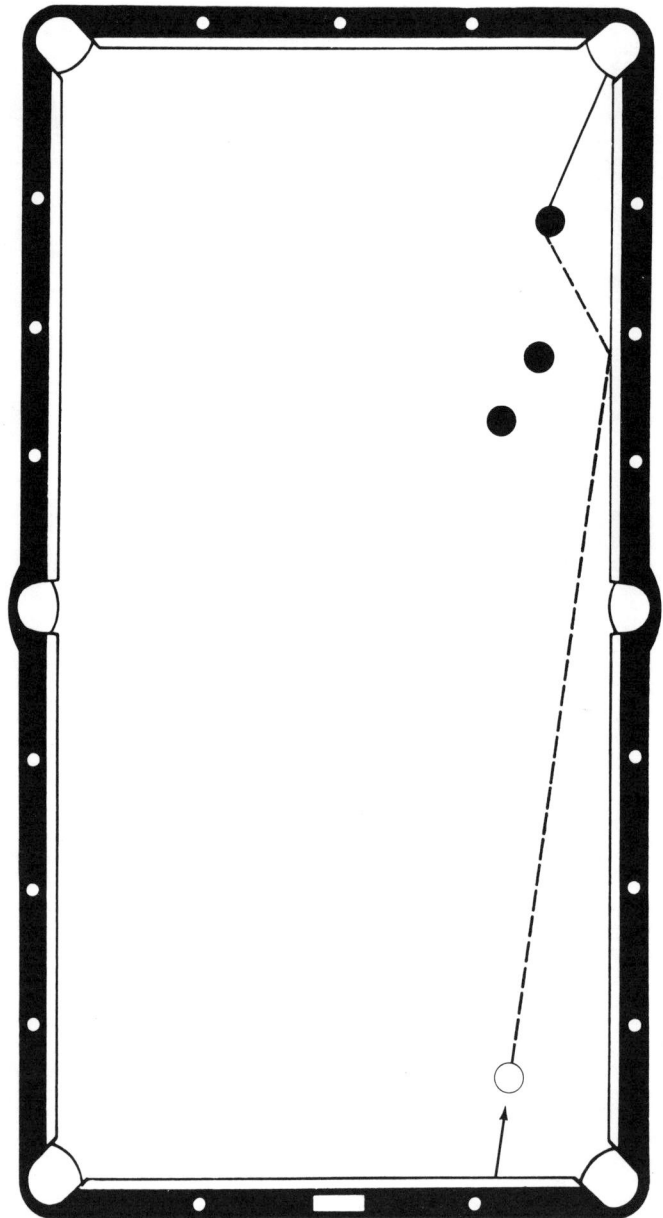

21. In a situation like this, the amateur might be tempted to try some kind of disastrous combination shot in the hope of sinking something! This one cushion shot is a sneaky way of getting around the problem. Unlike the billiards player, the pool player too often thinks of the cushion merely as a playing boundary rather than as a useful tool in difficult situations.

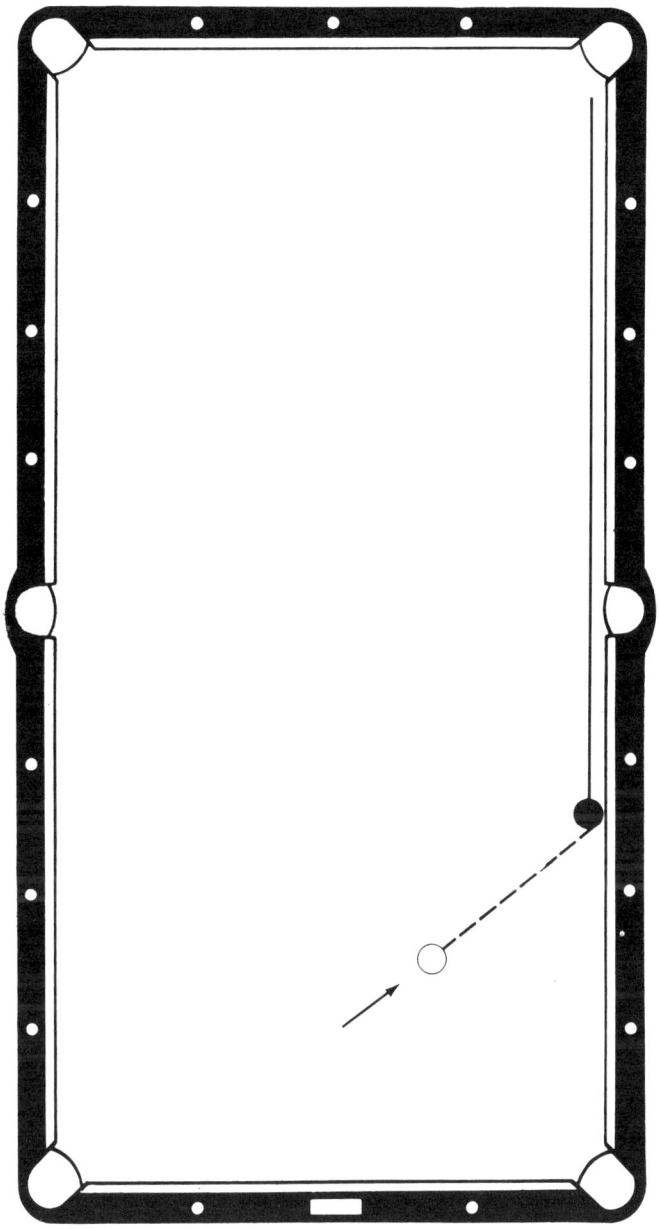

22. Here the object ball is frozen on the rail. This type of cut shot requires a good eye and should be practiced a great deal.

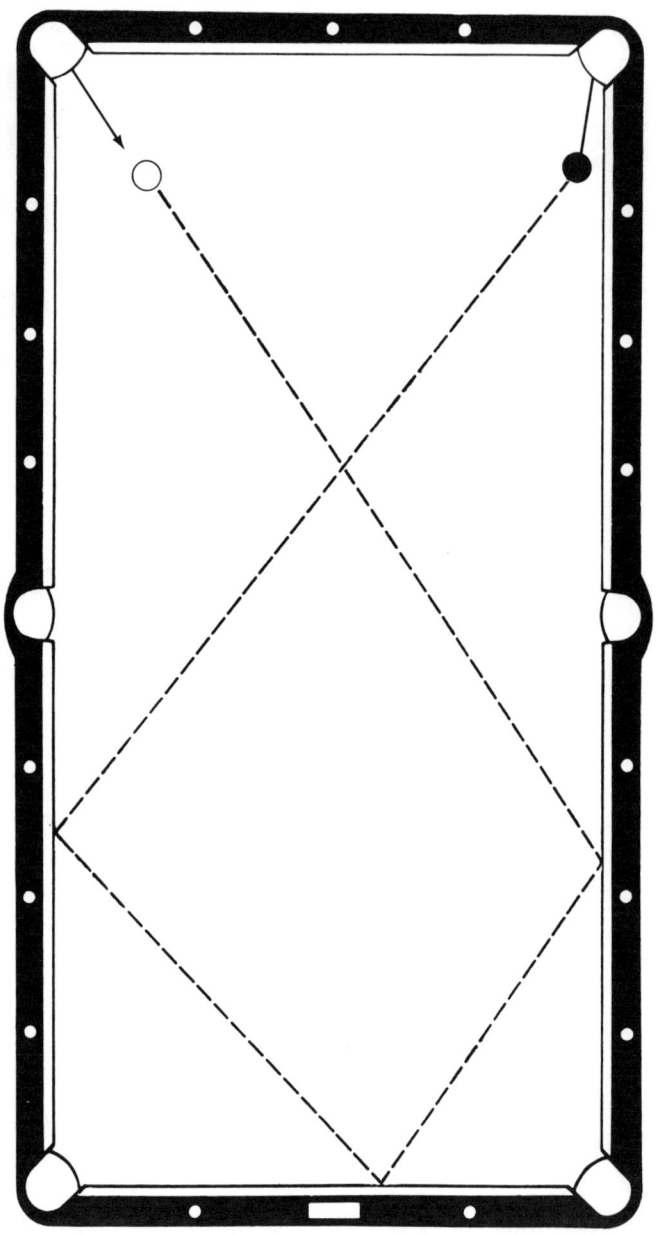

23. This three-cushion shot, which looks like it more properly belongs on a billiard table than a pool table, requires a fairly sophisticated understanding of table geometry, but it has solved the problem of how to put the object ball in the corner pocket.

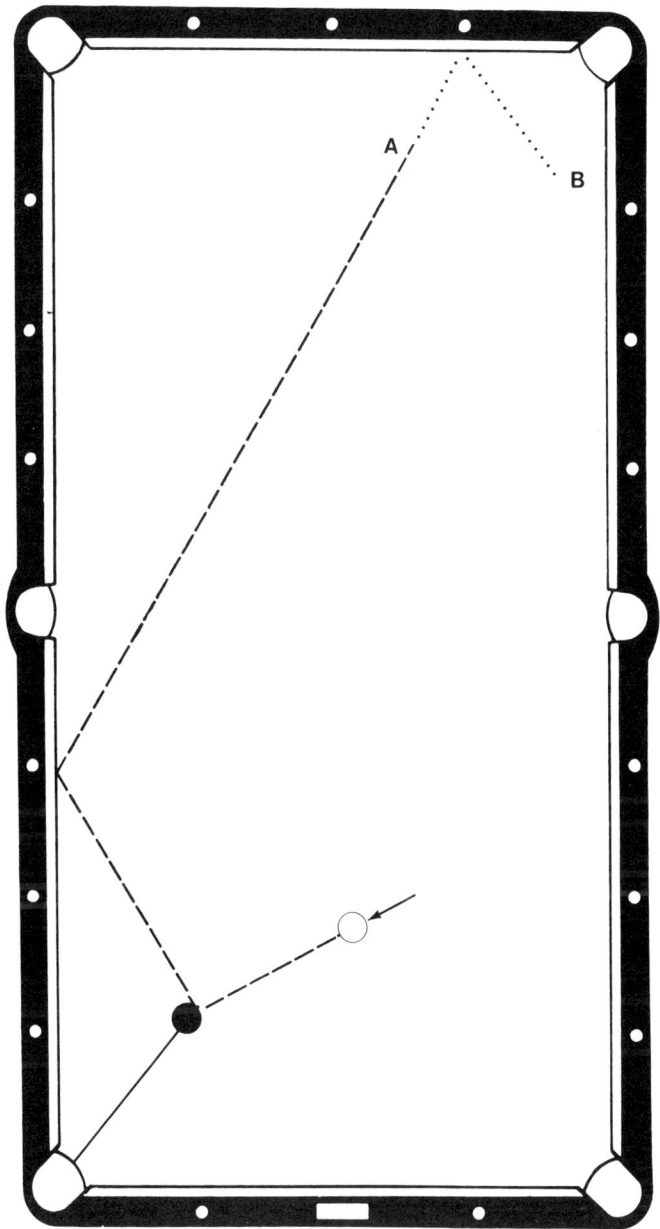

24. Sometimes it is necessary to be able to move the cue ball to the opposite side of the table, and a good player should know how to do this from a variety of situations. Slight draw is used on this cut shot, and the cue ball should finish up somewhere between A and B, depending on the strength of the stroke. The next object ball along the far cushion should present no problem.

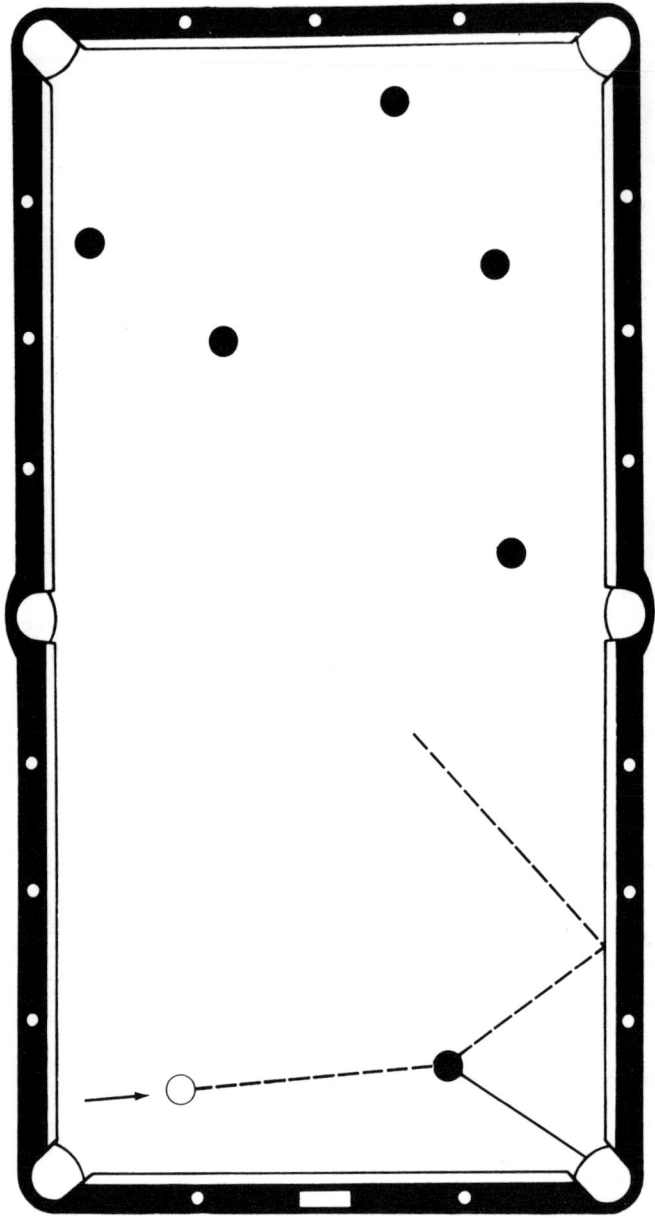

25. Here is an exercise involving six balls. Shoot a run of five and have yourself properly positioned for the next break. Such an exercise puts into practice many of the fundamentals shown in the other diagrams, but it does so in a context of greater complexity resembling a real game. There is no one way to solve the problem; the real object here is, again, control of the cue ball.

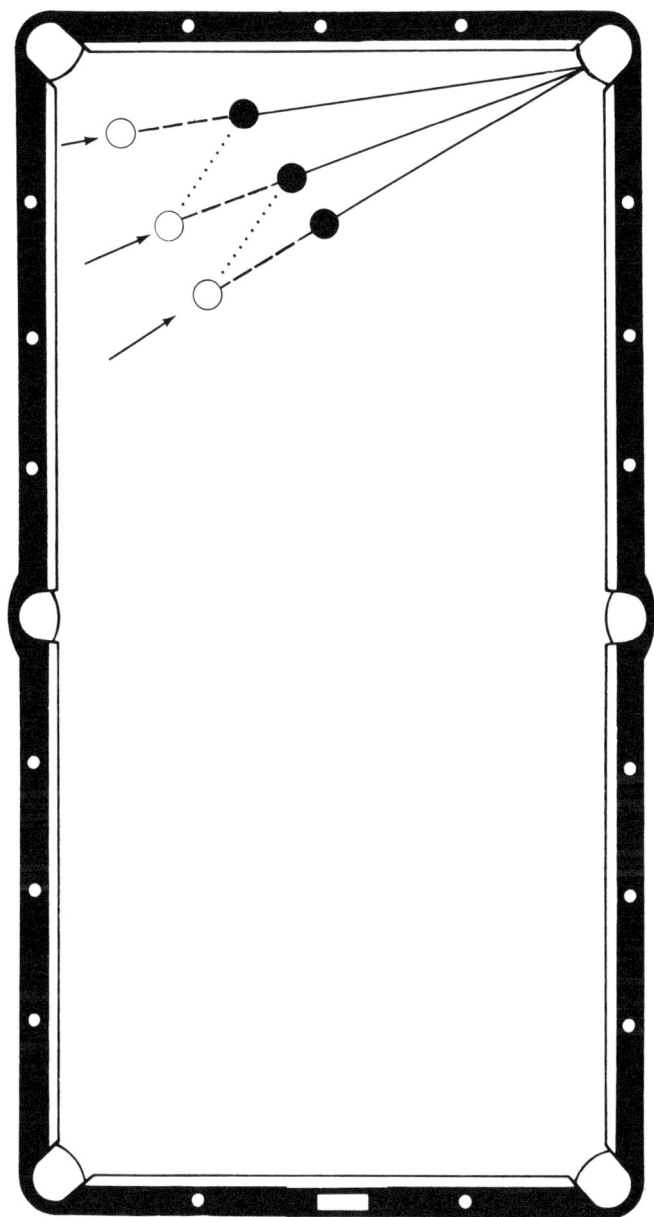

26. A series of light draw strokes with some right English will pocket these balls one after the other. Object balls often tend to accumulate at the ends of the table in actual play, so that the ability to shoot a run like this is important.

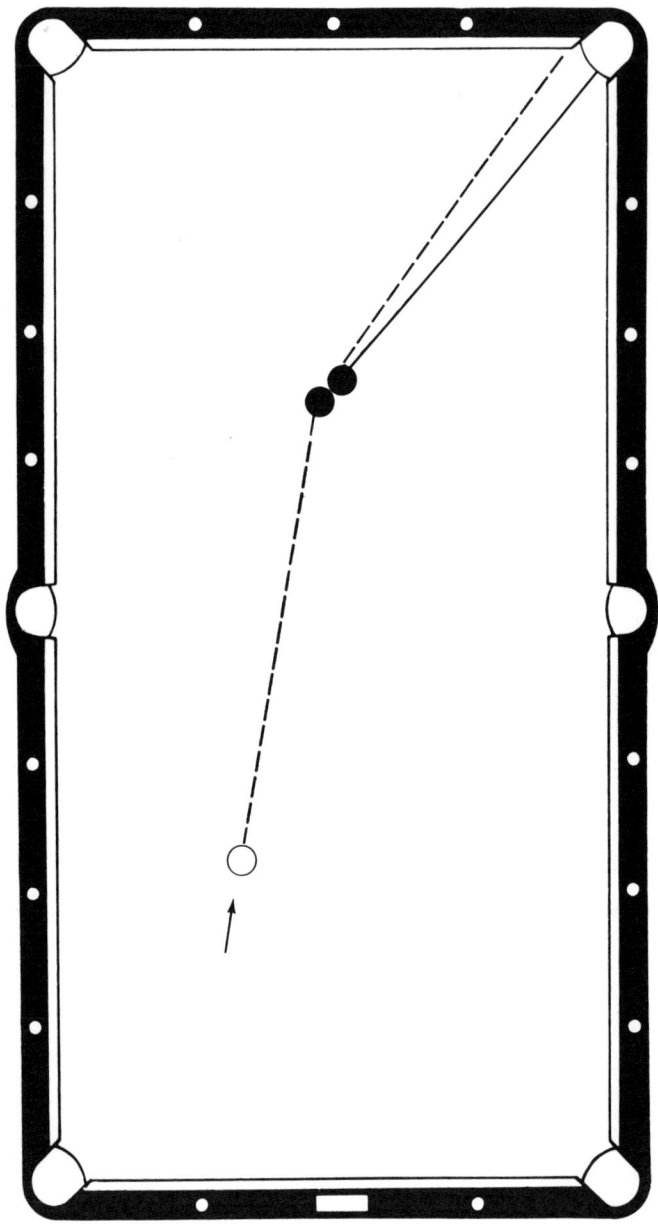

27. Here is an interesting combination shot involving two balls frozen together. The cue ball is hit dead center. The cut necessary to make this shot will impart English to the second object ball, and practice will teach the shooter how to compensate for the deflection, since a ball with English does not travel in a straight line. A good rule of thumb is 6 inches of deflection for every 36 inches of travel.

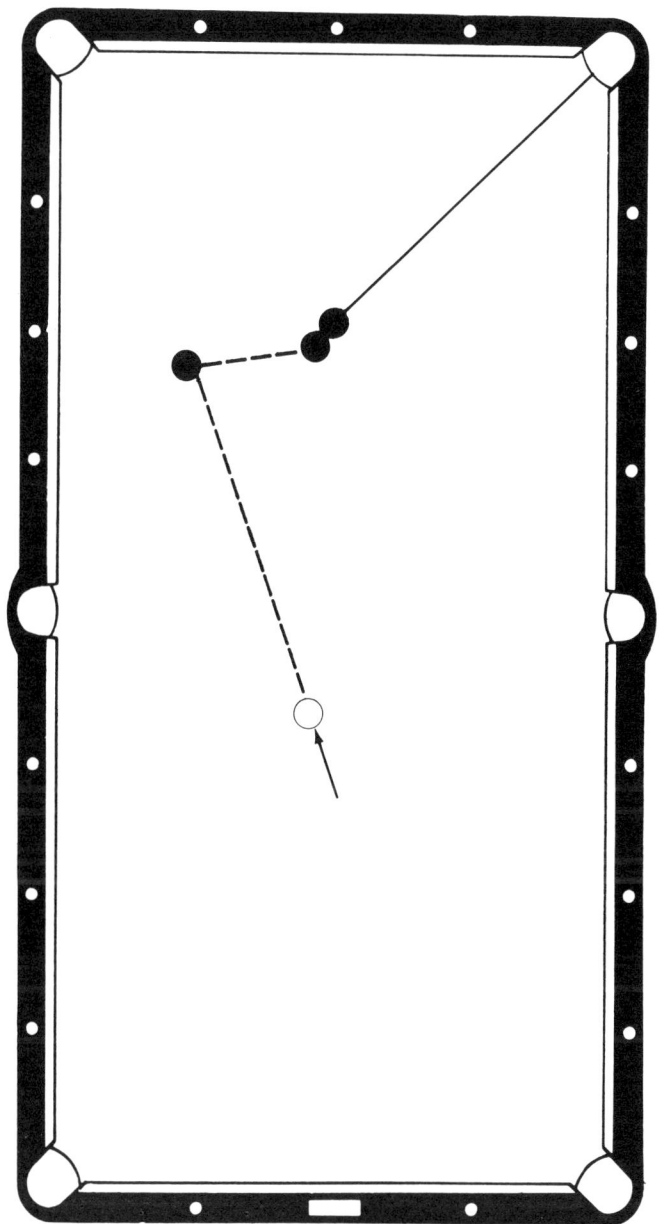

28. This fancy shot can be described as caroming into a combination. It involves most of the skills you've developed, and requires great accuracy. If you can make shots like this one, you will probably never be at a loss for a workable combination on the table. Again, you must allow for the deflection caused by left English imparted to the second object ball.

Billiards

Billiards is, of course, a very different game from pool. The table has no pockets—only a cue ball and two object balls are used—and the game involves mastering the complicated geometry of hitting both object balls and a specific number of cushions as well. There are many different games of billiards. Straight billiards involves simply caroming from ball to ball, and whether or not any cushions are struck at all is unimportant as long as both object balls are hit. It would be well worthwhile to practice straight billiards before going on to more advanced games, as this will teach the beginner the fundamental problems of all billiard games.

Three-Cushion Billiards

The billiards game to which we will devote most of our attention is known as Three-Cushion Billiards or Three-Cushion Caroms. Here the player is required to hit three or more cushions either before or after hitting the first object ball. The sequence of events can vary quite a bit here. The cue ball may strike one or more cushions before hitting the first object ball and the other cushions afterward, or all three cushions before or after the first object ball, as long as three cushions are struck before the second object ball is hit. Given the rules of the game, there are two basic types of shots to be made. With a **carom shot** the cue ball is directed at an object ball and rebounds into the cushions. With a **bank shot** the cue ball is directed against a cushion first and rebounds into an object ball.

Billiard Diagrams

The 5 System

The essence of billiards, even more so than pool, is knowledge of table geometry and ball trajectory. Developing this knowledge is less exasperating than the beginner might think. Diagram 29 will introduce you to the 5 system, an ingenious and practical aid to knowing where to shoot. Systems, of course, are only guides and are not infallible. Table surfaces may vary with changes in temperature and humidity. Tables may not be made properly to begin with, or they may not be correctly installed and leveled. And if the shooter does not have a smooth, even stroke, the system is worthless. All this must be borne in mind. Remember too that the object of most billiard games is not only to strike the two object balls, but to strike three cushions as well. This is fundamental to the system.

Stand at one of the short rails of the table and imagine that the diamonds, or points, along those rails are numbered. Whichever short rail you choose, the corners nearest you begin with the number 5 and decrease by half units as you look down the table. The numbers also extend around your rail to a maximum of 8, though on the short rail the diamonds represent whole units. Now study the two shots illustrated very carefully. **If you shoot toward the far end of the table from a specific point, and if you count subdivisions from the far end of the table to the rebound points on both long rails, you will discover that the total number of subdivisions equals the number of the point from**

which the shot was made. Thus a shot from the 5 corner aimed two points away from the far rail must strike the third cushion it hits three points from the far rail. A shot from 3 striking the first cushion one point down will strike the third cushion two points down. Do not confuse the numbers themselves with the number of subdivisions. This is really all there is to it, and it doesn't take much imagination to see that wherever the object balls are in relation to the cue ball, there is a way of getting at them and hitting the requisite number of cushions as well.

It's important to bear in mind that **with the 5 system the first cushion struck is always a long one.** The position of the shooter is known as the **starting point.** The spot struck on the first rail is known as the **striking point,** and the spot struck on the third cushion is known as the **scoring point.** A simple way of remembering the 5 system is to say that the striking point plus the scoring point equals the starting point.

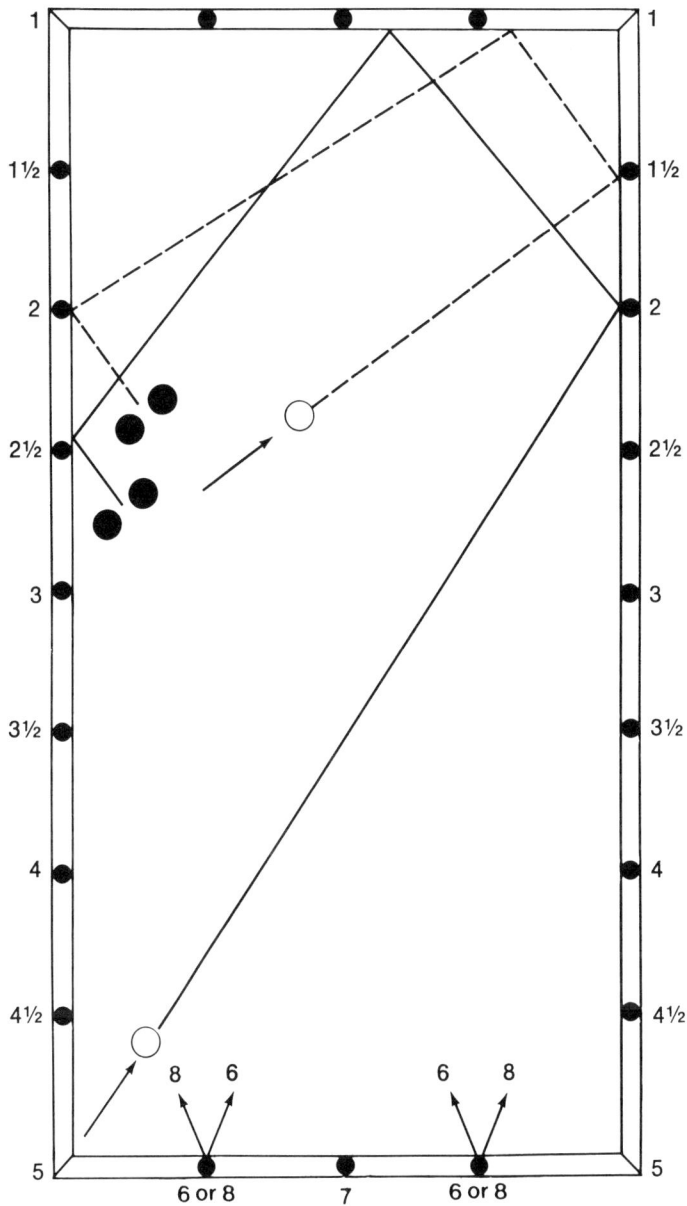

29. The 5 system.

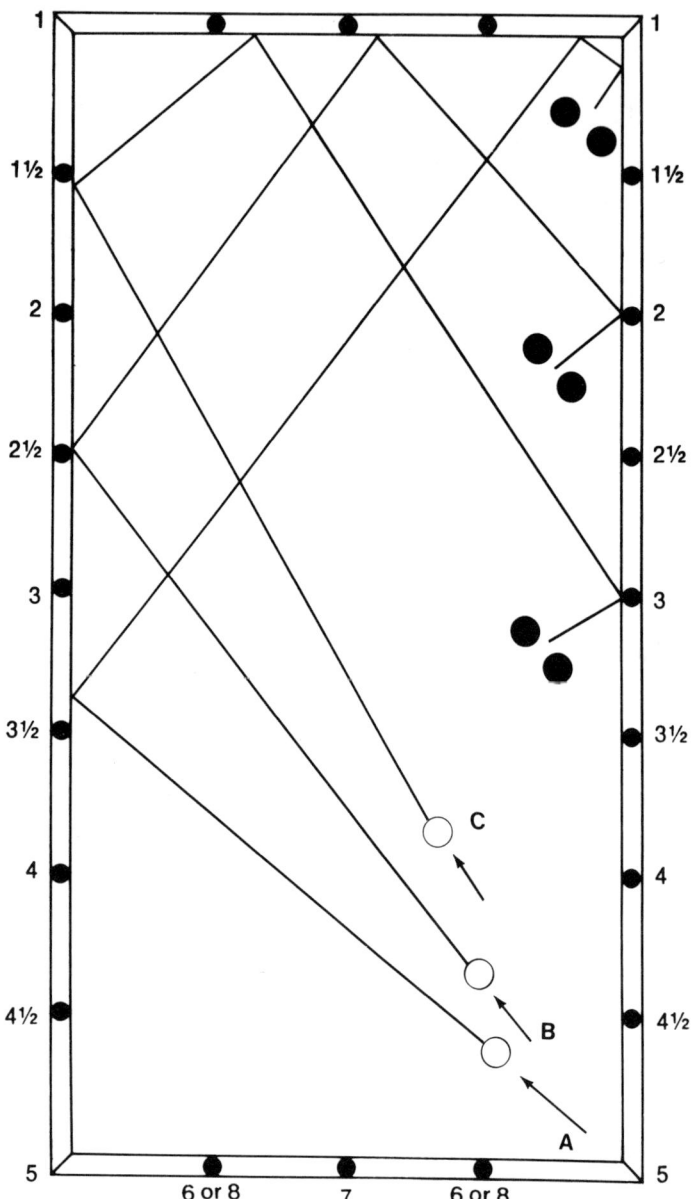

30. This diagram also illustrates the basic principle of the 5 system with three shots beginning from the same corner point. The first shot, A, is aimed four and three-quarter units from the far rail and hence strikes the third rail only one-quarter unit down. This is close to the limit of the system in this respect. If you were to aim more than five units down on the first rail, the cue ball would not strike three consecutive cushions and would in fact miss the short cushion completely. Notice the changing geometry in B and C, and how as the aiming point along the first cushion moves up toward the far rail, it moves down along the third cushion.

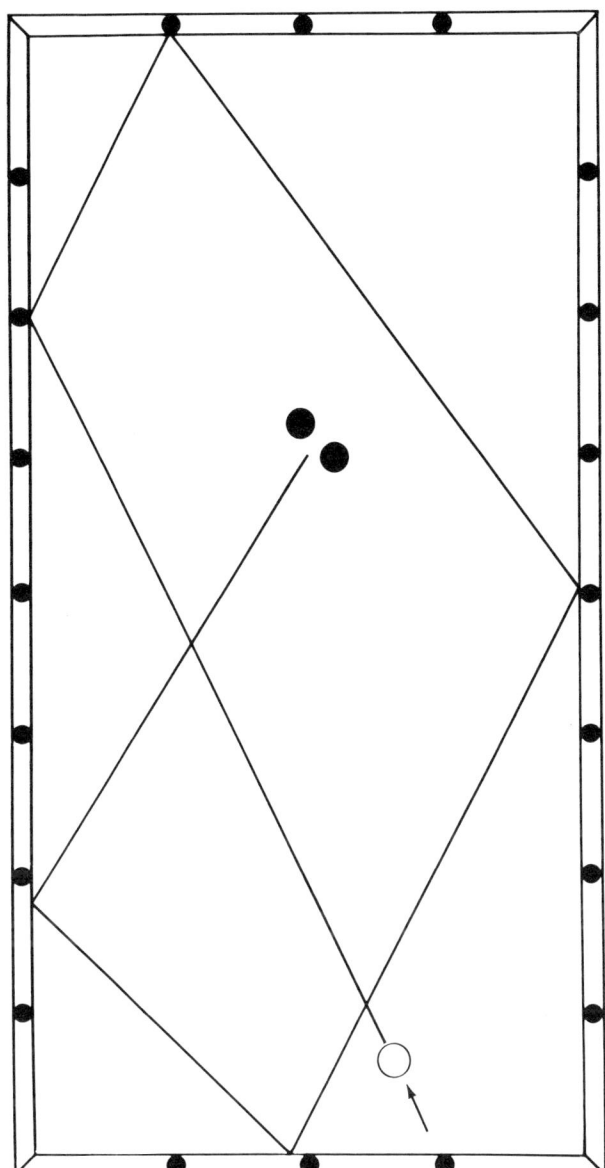

31. To prevent you from becoming rigid or mechanical in your thinking about this system, the diamonds on the remaining diagrams will not be numbered, and, of course, not all shots will be made from the bottom of the page. In this five-cushion bank shot the starting point is one of the 6/8 points on the short rail. If you are shooting from this position across the greater width of the table, across the 7 point, the significant number is 6. If you are shooting across the lesser width of the table, toward the nearest long rail, the significant number is 8. The starting point here, then, is 6, and if the ball is aimed two points away from the far rail it will rebound off the fourth point on the third cushion. If the cue ball is hit hard enough, it will go on to hit a fourth and fifth cushion. Note that the track from the fourth to the fifth cushion will form the base of an isosceles triangle.

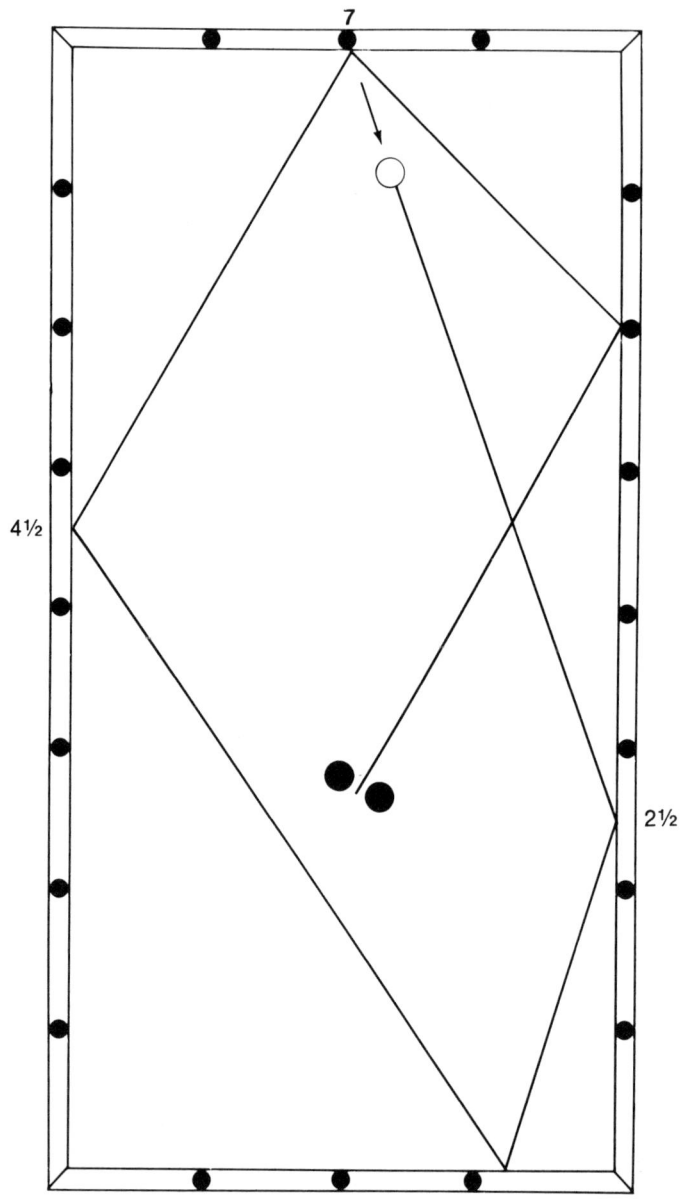

32. Here is a five-cushion bank shot starting from 7. Again one can see that the bank points add up to 7, and that the track from the fourth to the fifth cushion forms an isosceles triangle.

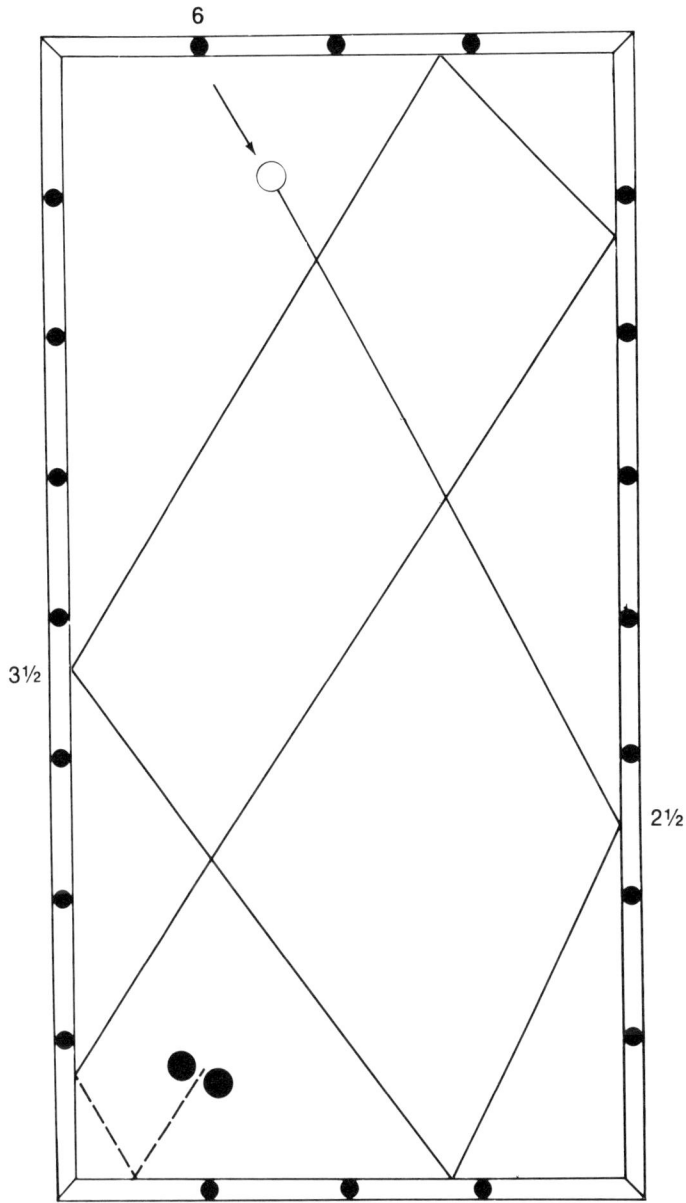

33. This seven-cushion shot demonstrates how one might actually work backwards from the object balls to the cue ball. We decide that we are going to come at the object balls from "behind" using the near corner. The dotted line is known as the backup. From the sixth cushion to the fifth cushion, the distances of the contact points from the short rails must add up to 2. The line from the fifth to the fourth cushion will form an isosceles triangle. From the fourth cushion to the third cushion takes us to the scoring point, and from this point we apply the rules for the 5 system.

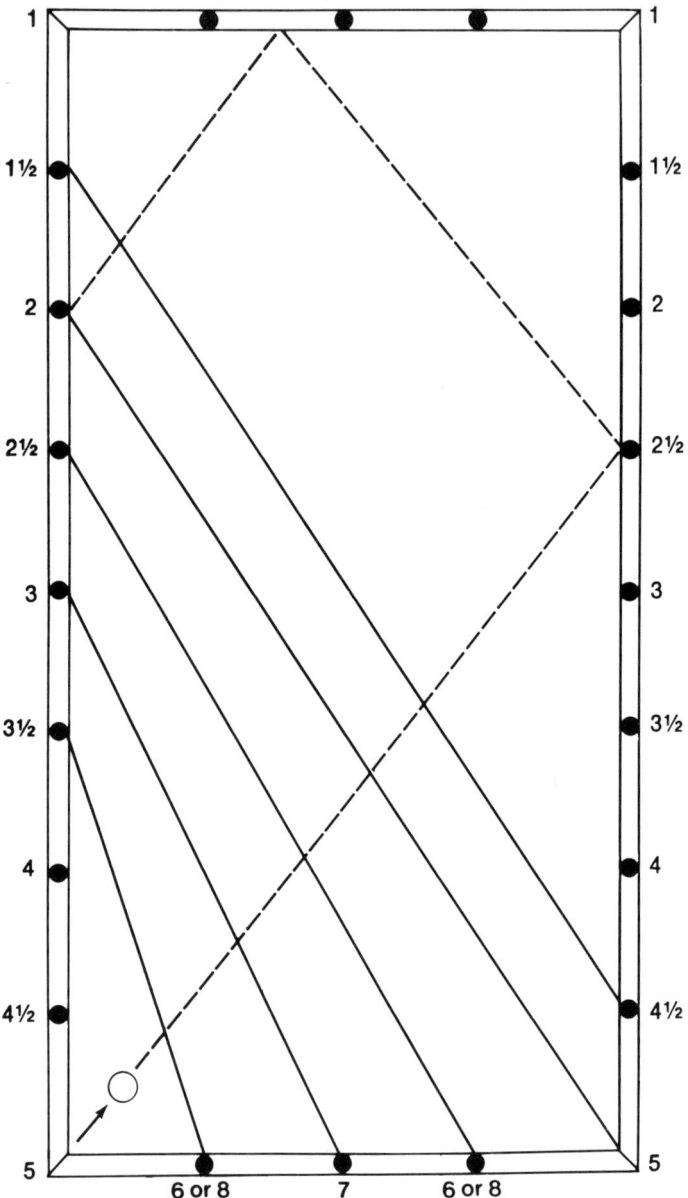

34. While the system for the first three cushions of the 5 system follows a neat mathematical rule, to extend the track of the cue ball beyond that point to the fourth cushion requires that the player fix in his mind certain links between specific points or diamonds. Using the 5 system, the shooter discovers that the first diamond down the third rail is connected to the first diamond up from the other side of the table along the fourth rail. The second point on the third cushion is connected to the corner point on the opposite rail, the third point down is connected to the 6/8 diamond, and so on. With these connecting points memorized, one can extend three-cushion shots to four or more cushions. A four-cushion shot with a scoring point of 2 is shown.

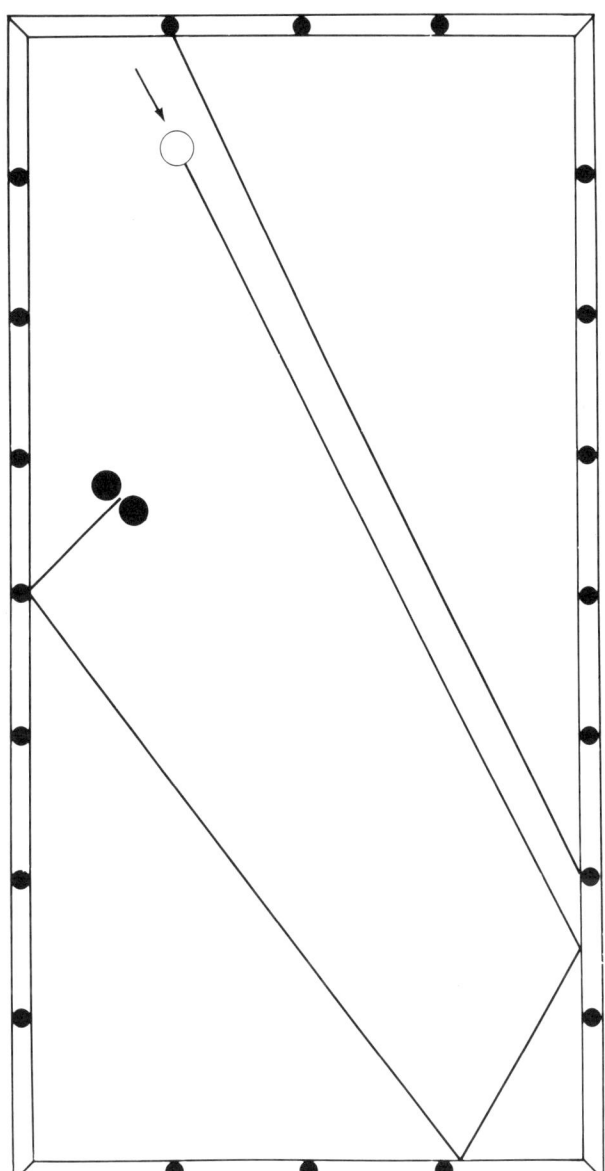

35. This diagram introduces the important principle of *parallels.* It will become evident shortly that the scoring point, the point of contact on the third cushion, is very important in terms of planning a shot. Suppose that you want the cue ball to rebound off a particular point on the third cushion, but your alignment is not perfect. In this instance you want to hit the midpoint on the third cushion, the 3 point. The line drawn between 6 and 4 represents the perfect line to the first cushion in order to hit 4 units down on the third cushion. But the cue ball is not on that line. Let's examine what happens if you shoot along a line that runs parallel to the perfect line. The cue ball is hit from a point with the numerical value of, say, 5¾. It will strike the first cushion at a point 1¾ units from the far end of the table. Since the striking point (1¾) plus the scoring point must equal the starting point (5¾), then the scoring point must be 4 units away from the far rail. The parallel, in other words, strikes the same point on the third cushion that the perfect 6 line would strike.

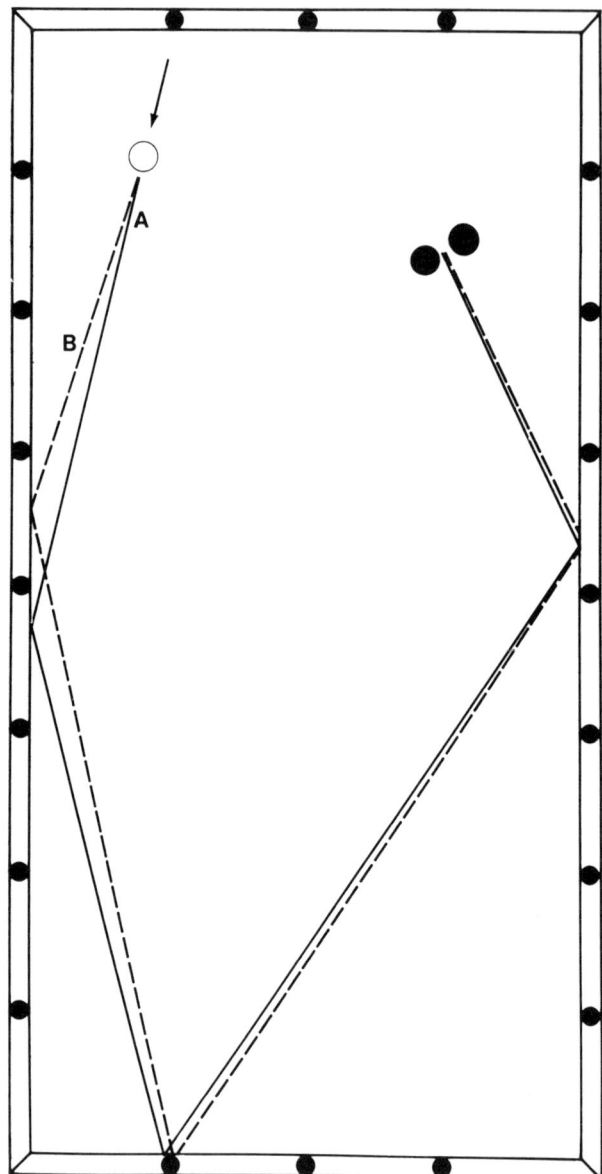

36. Now that the reader has become acquainted with the basic geometry of billiards, it must be said that rules can only take one so far, and after that experience and judgment are what distinguish the good from the great. Inexactnesses exist everywhere on a pool table, not the least of which is the nature and strength of one's stroke. In diagram 36, for example, the same shot is made in two different fashions. In *A*, the shooter has exploited the 5 system perfectly, but a forceful stroke is necessary. Less force is required for *B* if the striking point is moved closer to the shooter by one half to three quarters of the space between diamonds.

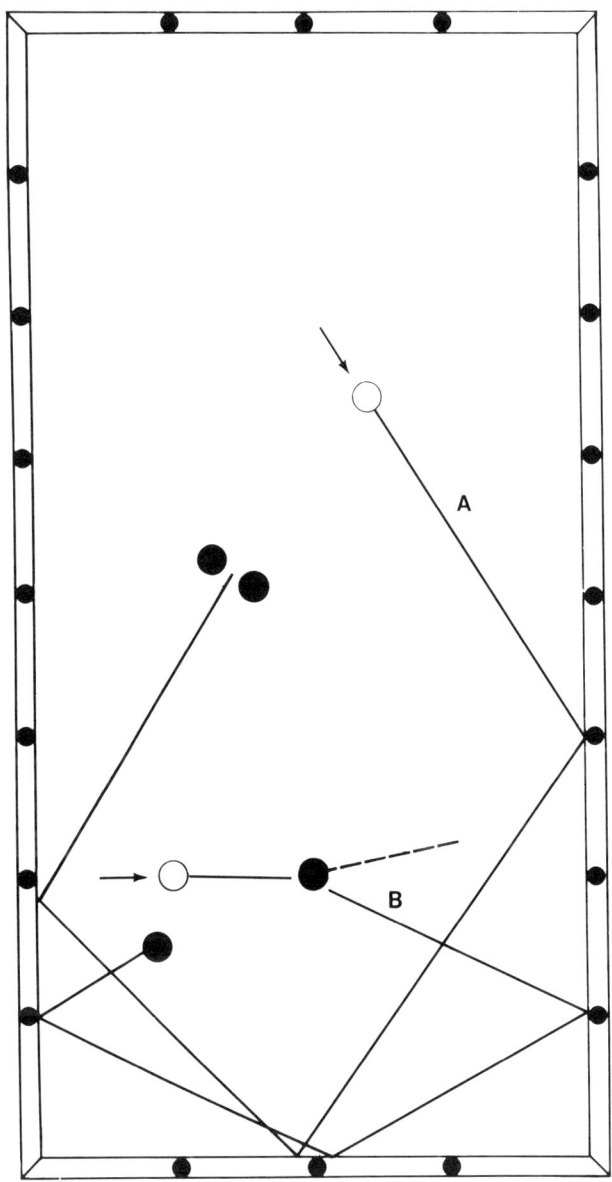

37. Trajectory A shows a bank-shot triangle. In trajectory B, the shooter caroms off the first object ball, making a perfect isosceles triangle between the first object ball and the points of contact on the first two cushions. No English is used on the cue ball for these shots.

The 2 System

38. Up to this point we have discussed the 5 system and we've noted that to use this system the cue ball must first be directed against a *long* rail. Another very useful system, deserving much study and practice, is the 2 or 2 plus system, and as one might expect, this is used when the cue ball is directed first against one of the short rails.

First the shooter mentally establishes a "base point" exactly halfway between the corner and the first diamond on the short rail. Using this as our aiming point, the following rule comes into play: the scoring point on the third cushion will be 2 diamonds down from the starting point. Trajectory *A* shows a perfect 2 plus shot, starting at 3, hitting the base point, and returning two diamonds down at 4. For the system to work properly, a stroke of medium force should be used, as well as one half a cue-tip width of English in the direction that the cue ball will bounce off the first cushion.

Trajectories *B* and *C* show how the system can be played with. If you want the cue ball to strike the third cushion *more* than two diamonds down, as in *B*, aim to the right of the base point. If you want the cue ball to strike the third cushion *less* than two diamonds down, as in *C*, aim to the left of the base point. In general, adjusting the aim by one half the distance between diamonds on the short rail modifies the distance on the third rail by one complete space between diamonds. The 2 system plus the 5 system opens up a whole new range of possible shots.

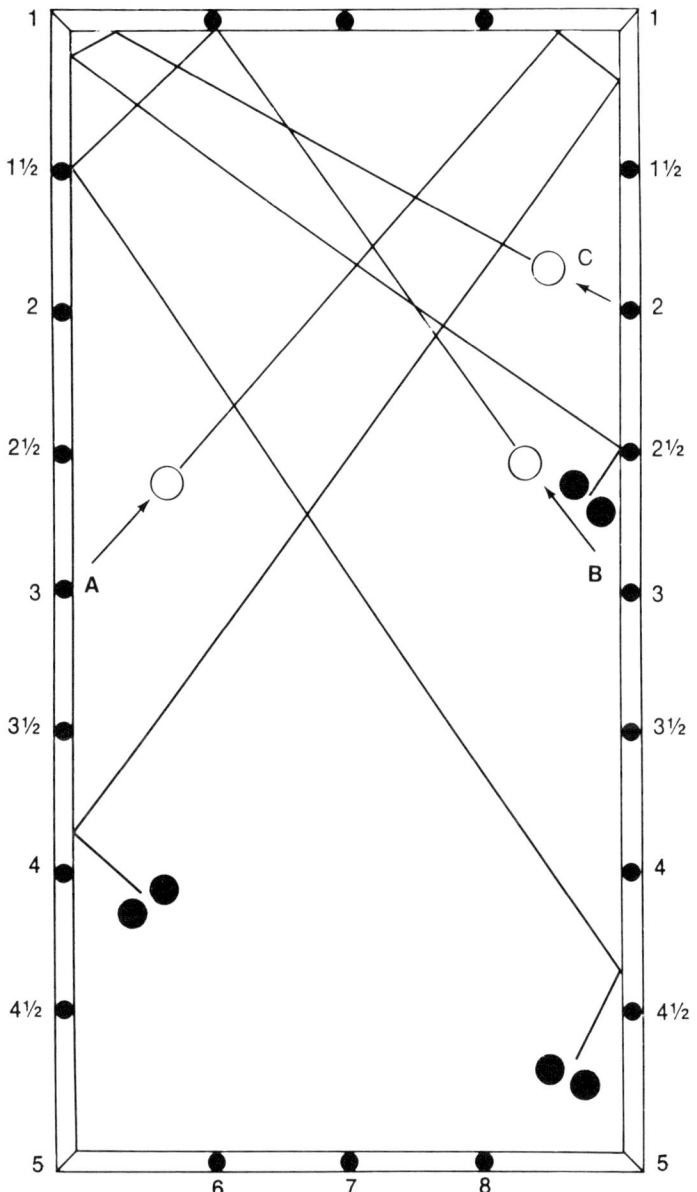

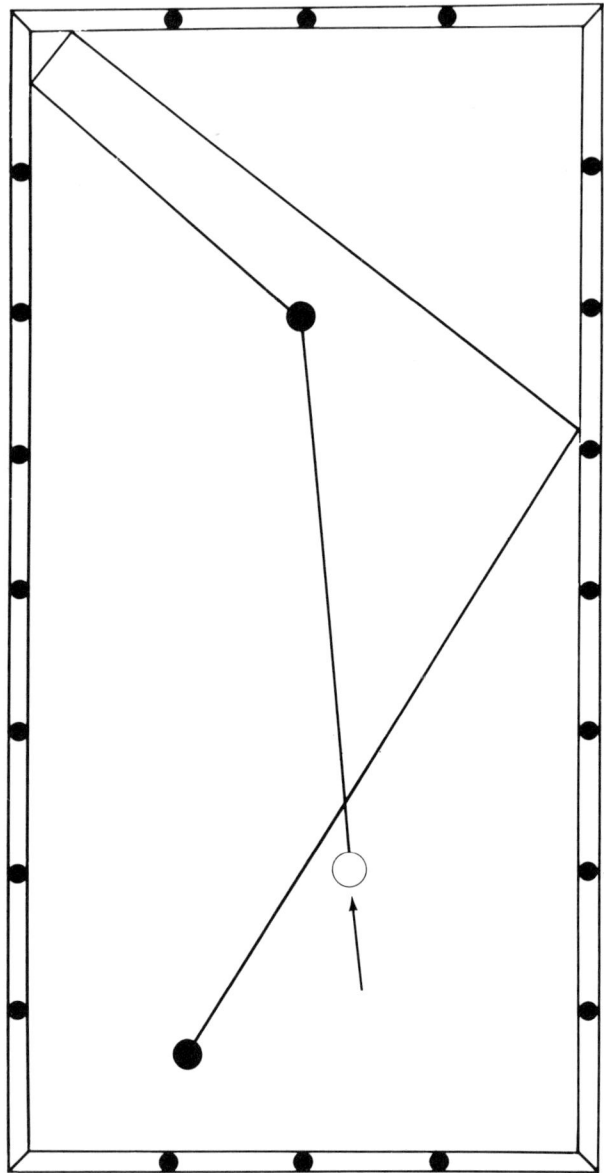

39. Undoubtedly the reader has been studying the preceding diagrams and wondering what happens when the two object balls are not conveniently situated next to each other, as will often be the case in an actual game. Well, of course, the possibilities are endless, but the key to such play is to re-create the basic geometry through careful and accurate caroming off the first object ball. The trajectory in this diagram is basically a 5 system shot made from a hypothetical starting point about three diamonds down from the short rail. But we must re-create the starting point from the first object ball. Use a stroke of medium force and one cue-tip width of English. Aim about one quarter of the object ball's width in.

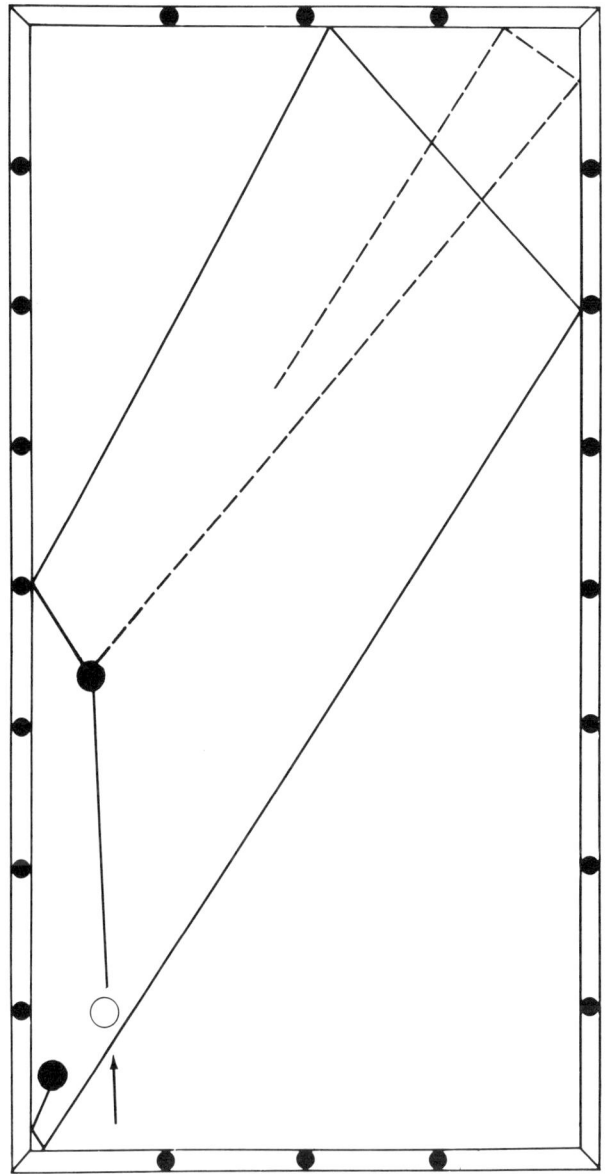

40. This is an interesting shot which can, by extension, be considered a 5-system shot from the 6 diamond on the short rail. An additional complication involves the problem of a possible collision between the cue ball and the first object ball.

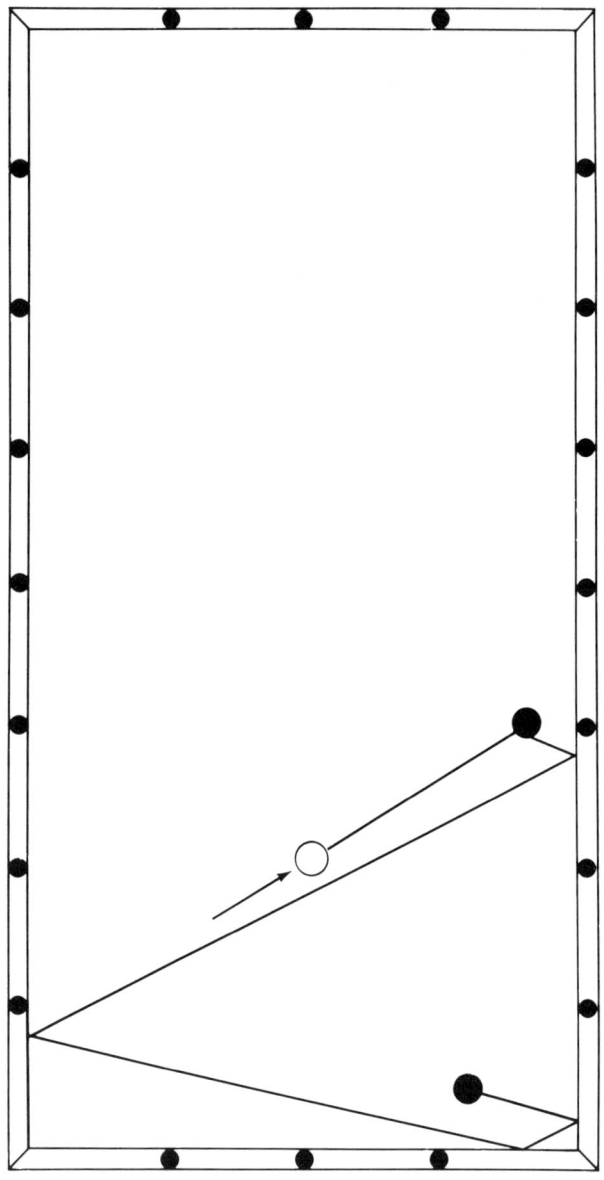

41. This cross-table shot requires a sharp stroke and some, but not too much, draw.

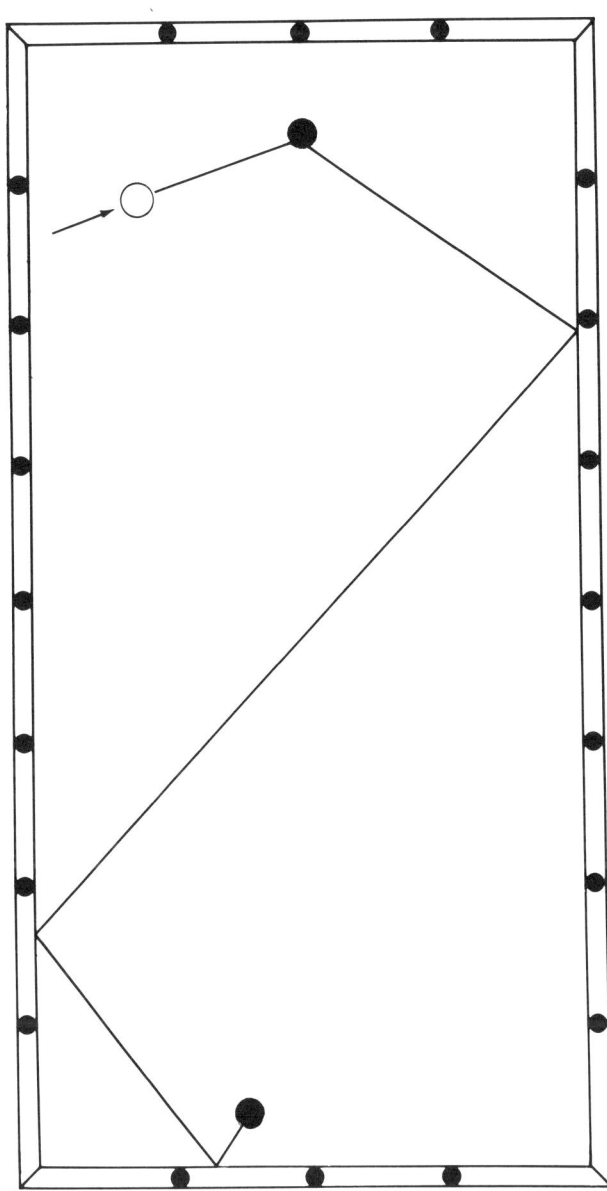

42. This shot is another exercise in placing the cue ball where you want to, and in learning how to carom off an object ball in a preplanned direction. The shooter should use just a half cue-tip width of draw.

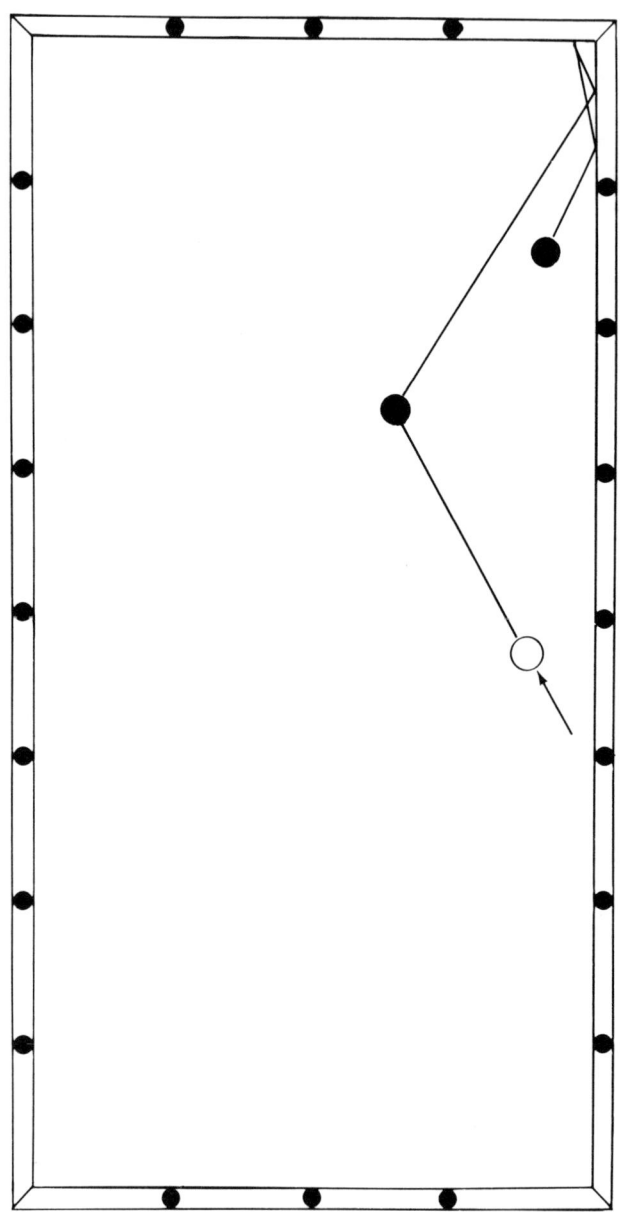

43. This carom shot is quite difficult and requires good control. The shooter uses just a touch of draw. In this case the shooter scores by hitting the same cushion twice. Double rail shots, as these shots are known, are not only permissible, but are very common in the course of a game.

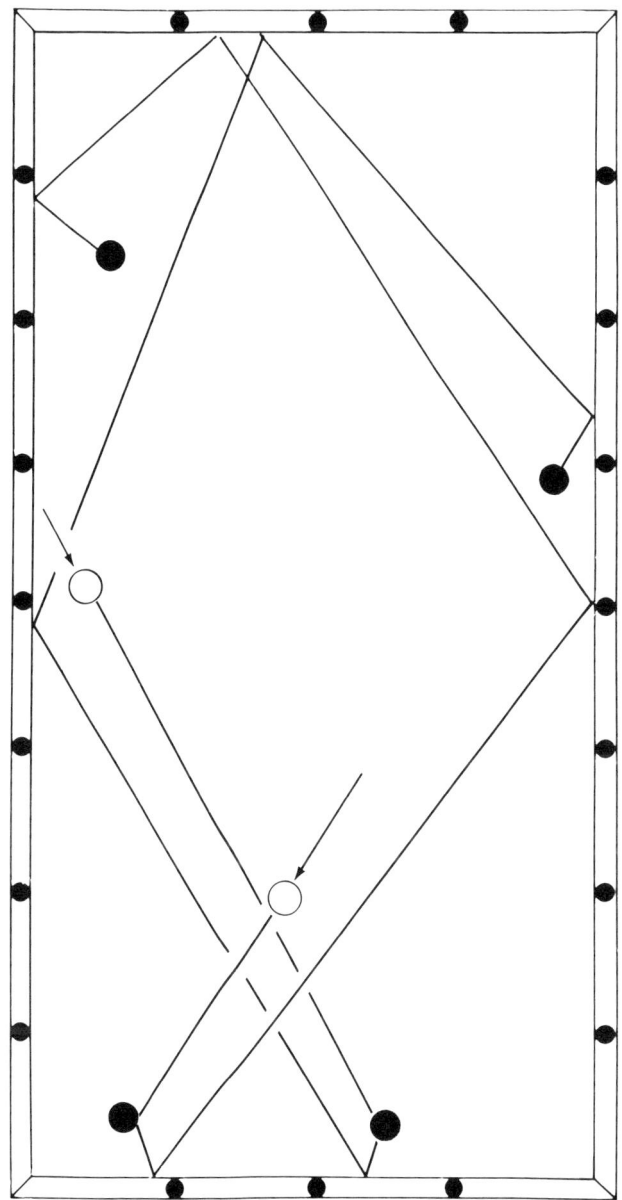

44. These two carom shots are made with one half a cue-tip width of draw. The idea is to pick a spot on the second cushion and carom off the object ball in such a way as to hit that spot.

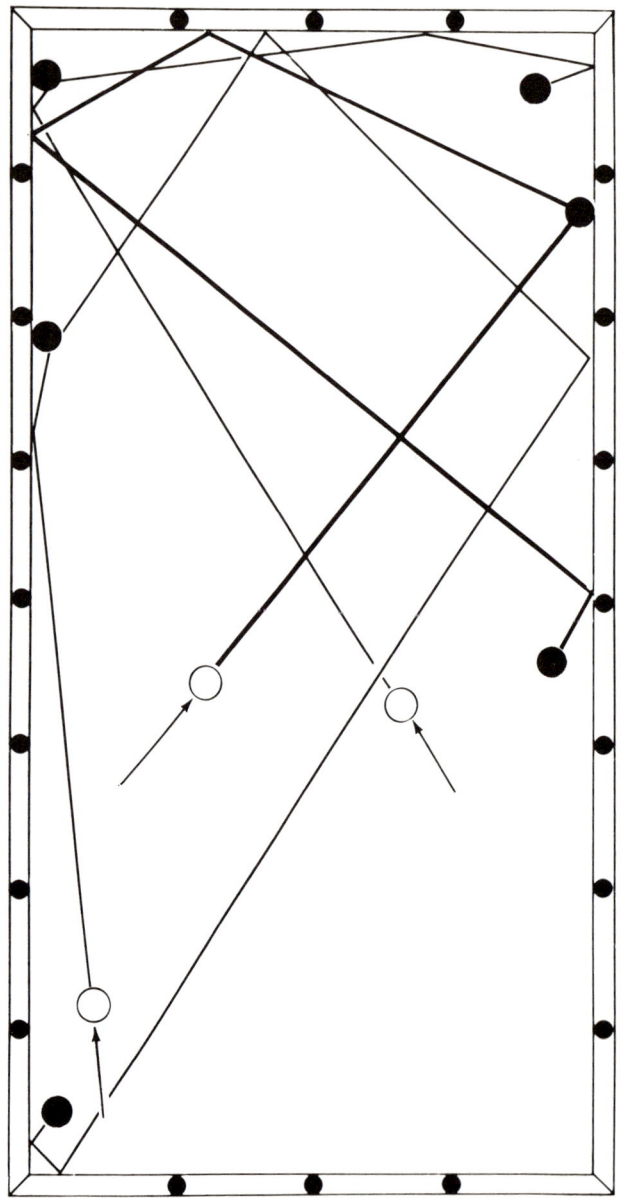

47. These three shots require quite a bit of experience, as they involve hitting the cushion first, and then carefully caroming off the object ball to alter the course of the cue ball.

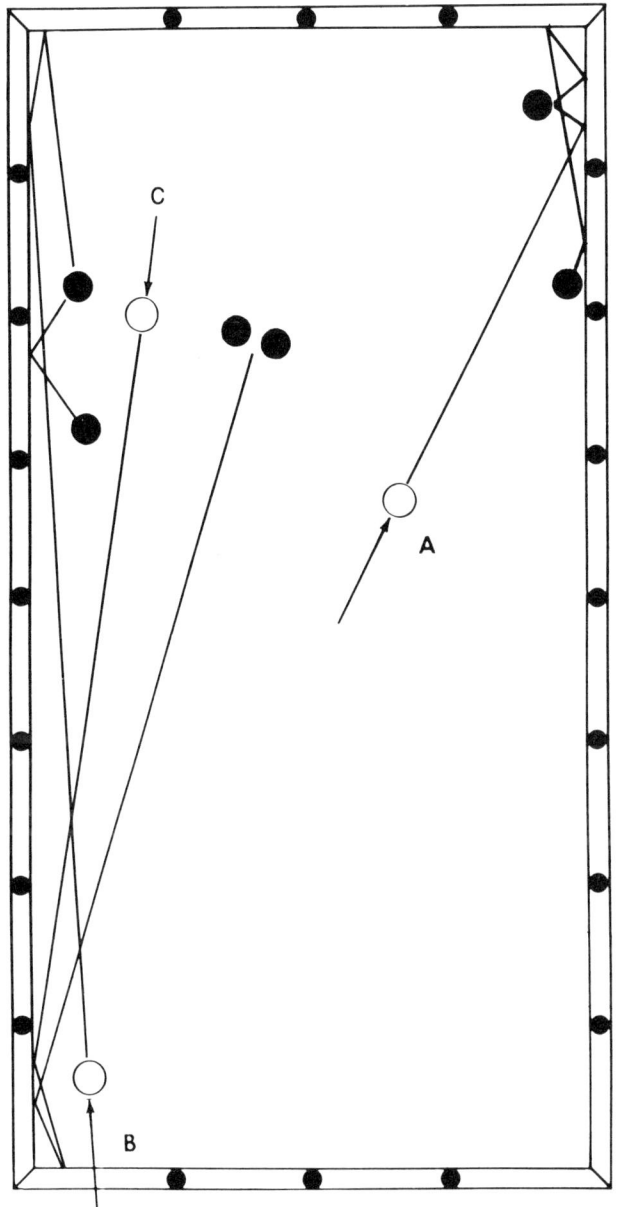

48. These three shots, begun somewhat greater distances from the object balls than in diagram 46, also demonstrate the difficult handling of the cue ball in the corner. *A* requires reverse English. *B* uses a center-ball stroke.

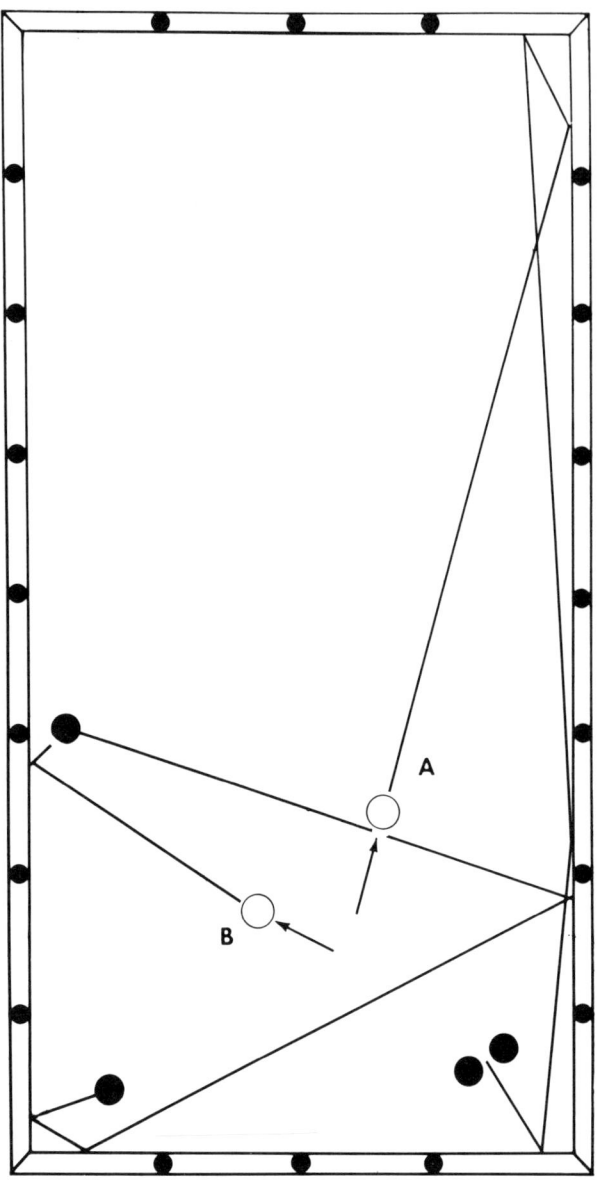

49. This diagram illustrates two more difficult shots that involve striking a cushion first and then caroming off an object ball. *A* goes to the long rail and then reverses itself. *B* is made with both draw and right English.

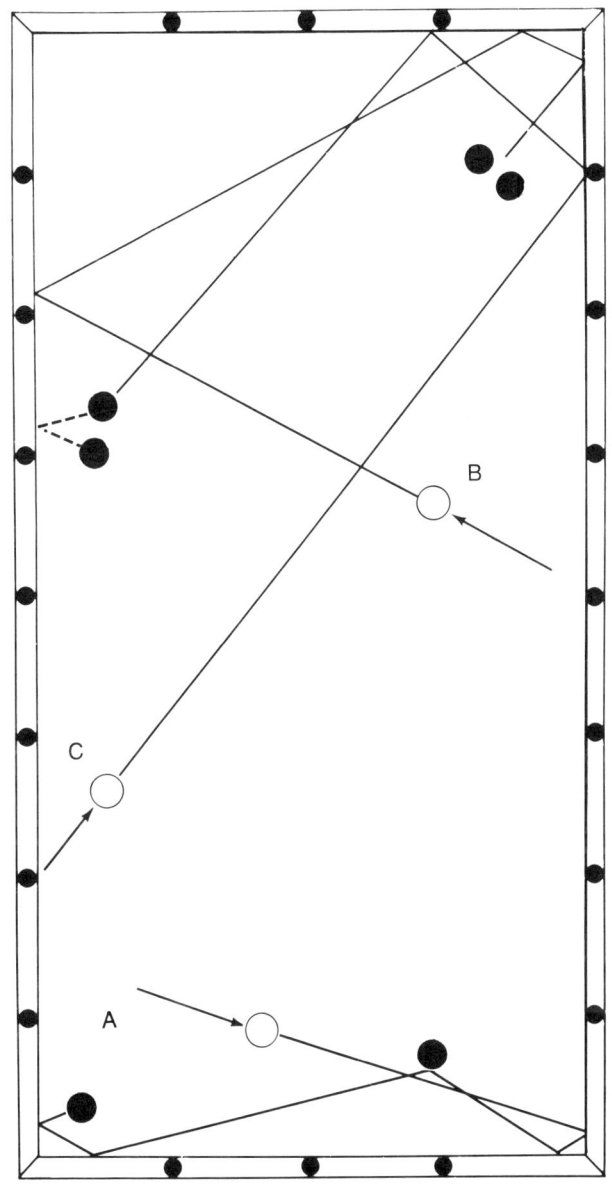

50. Here are three more shots that should be practiced. *A* strikes the long rail first. *B* is made with a center-ball stroke. *C* is known as an umbrella shot.

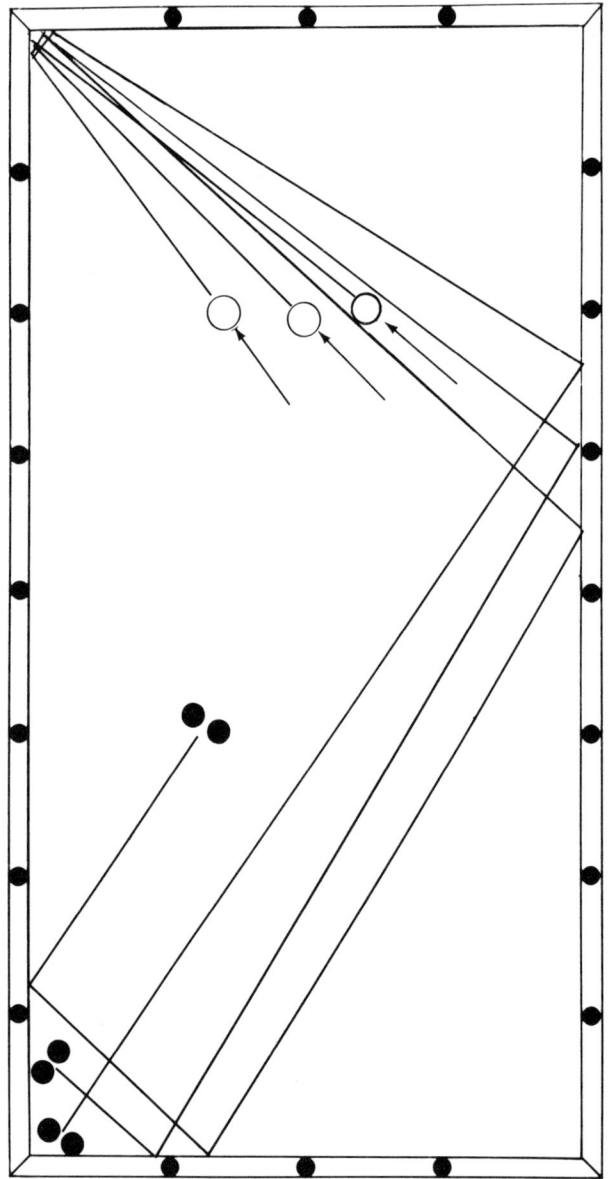

51. These three shots, all made from the upper points on the table, strike the long rail first and basically follow the 5 system. They demonstrate how slight changes in the position of the cue ball alter trajectories, as well as the range of possible positions for the object balls that can be hit under these circumstances.

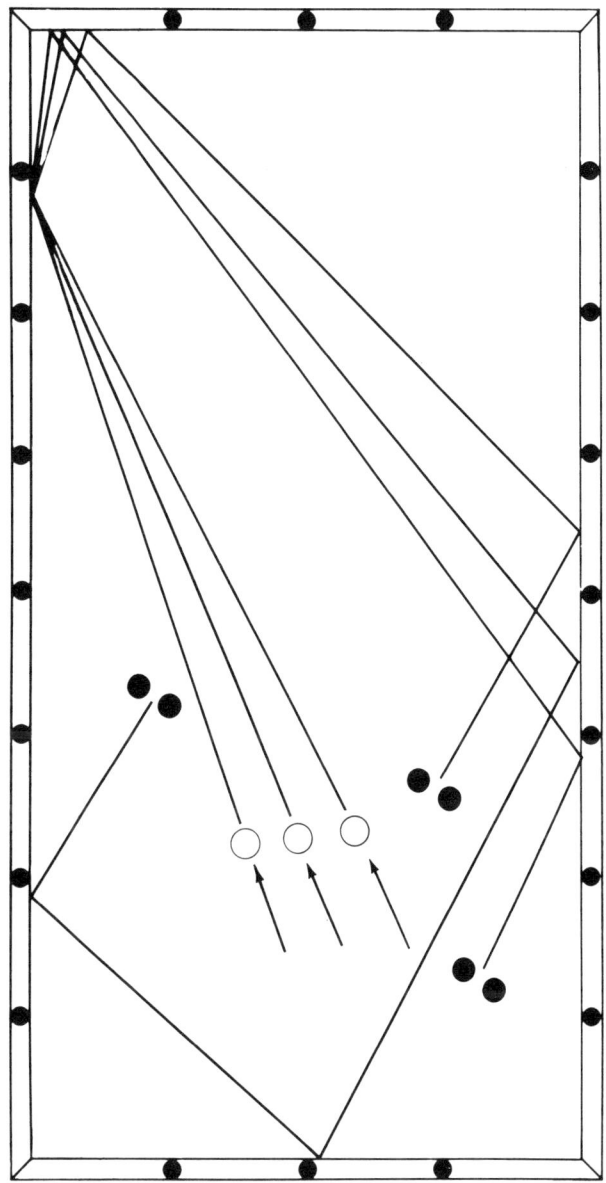

52. These three shots made from the lower points along the short rail also show the range of positions of object balls that can be tackled through slight variations in the placement of the cue ball.

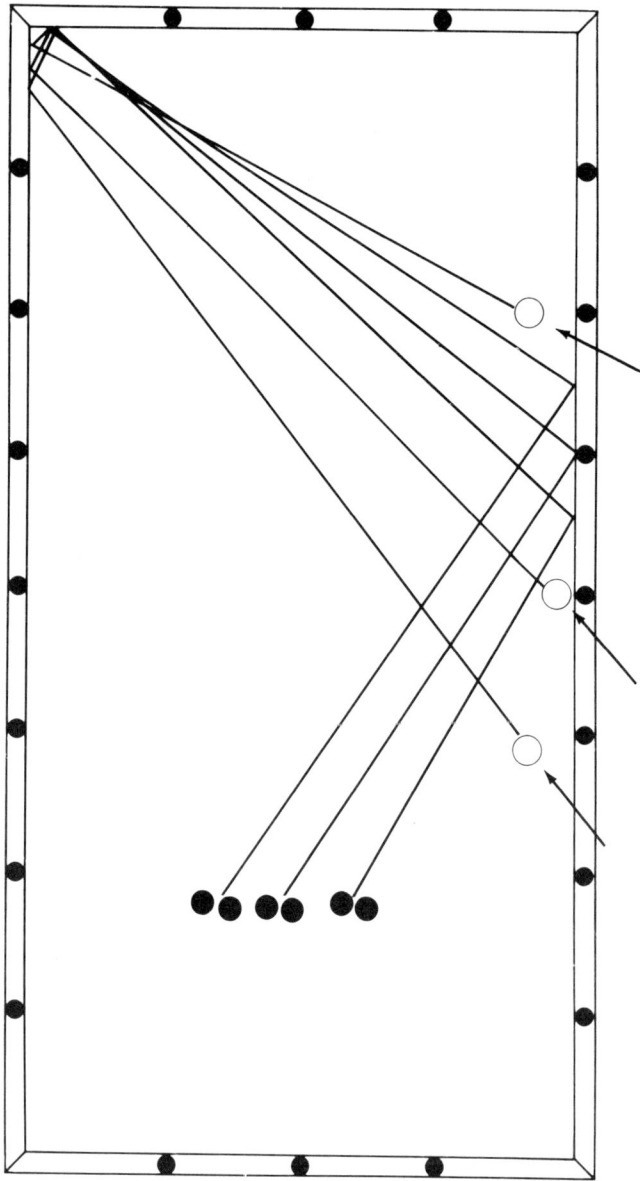

53. These three shots should be studied carefully. Though they are made from widely separated points, by varying slightly the striking point along the first cushion the trajectories can be brought closer together. Such adjustments enable the shooter to cover a whole area where the object balls might be located.

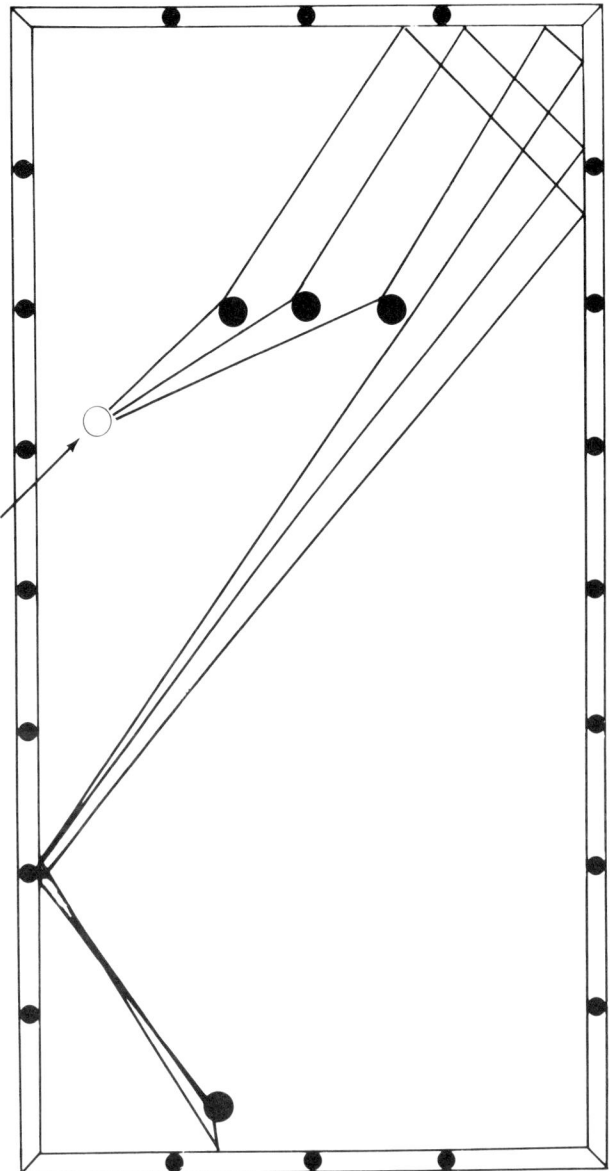

54. Again, these three shots, caroming off object balls in different positions, can be made to come together closely enough so that the second object ball will also be hit.

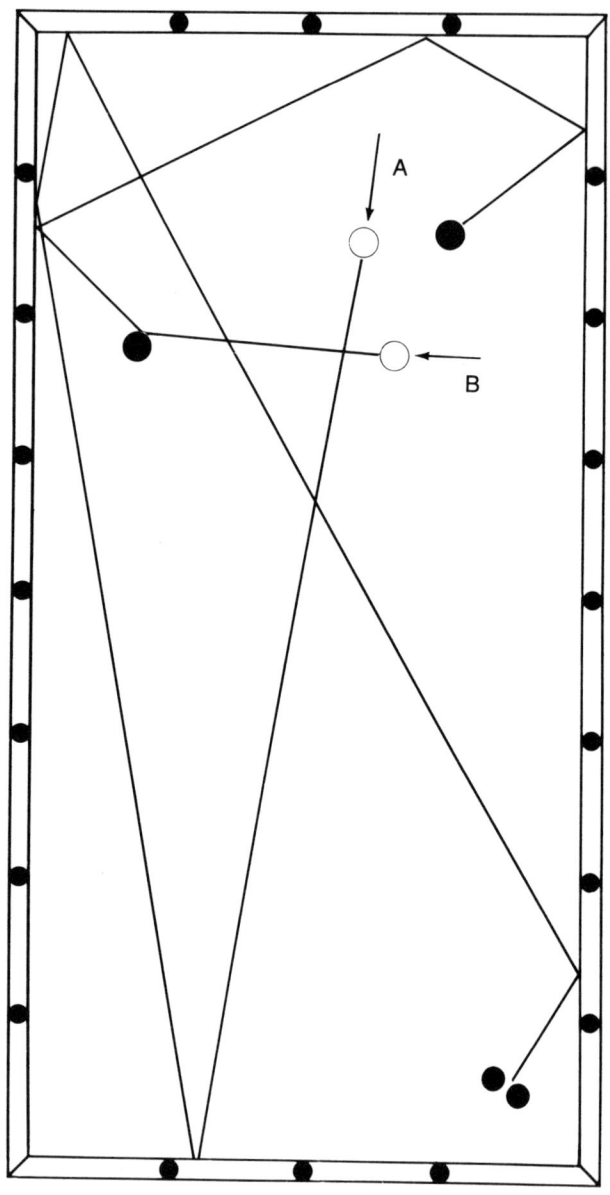

55. Trajectory A here is a four-cushion center-ball bank shot. B is an example of a center-ball carom shot.

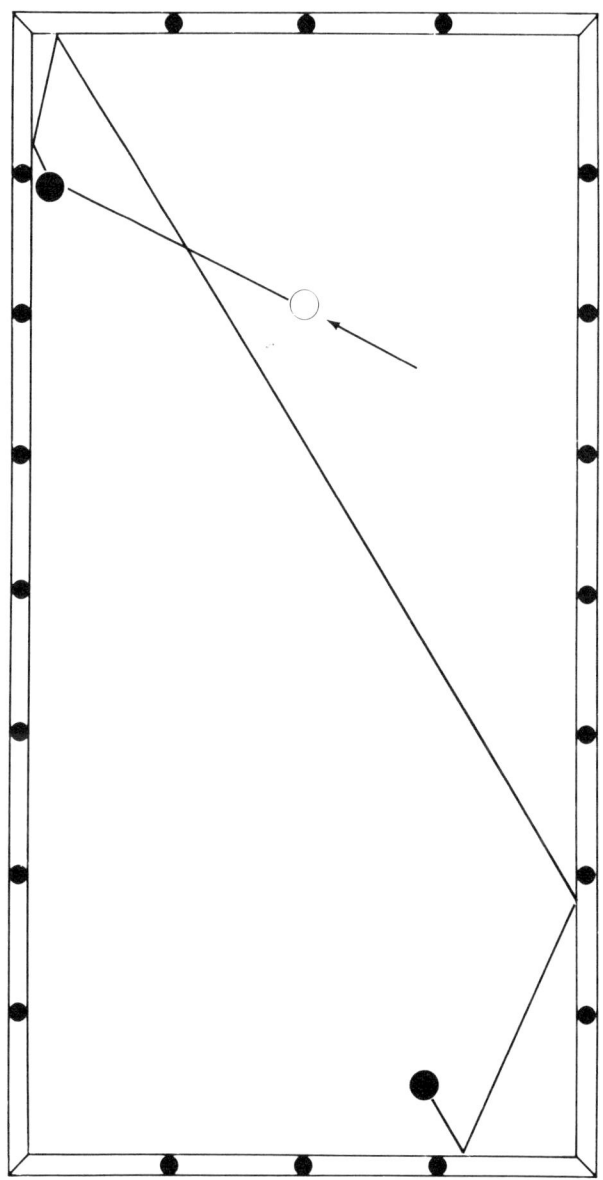

56. This center-ball carom shot is known as a high-ball hit. It requires precision timing to avoid having the rebounding object ball interfere with the roll of the cue ball.

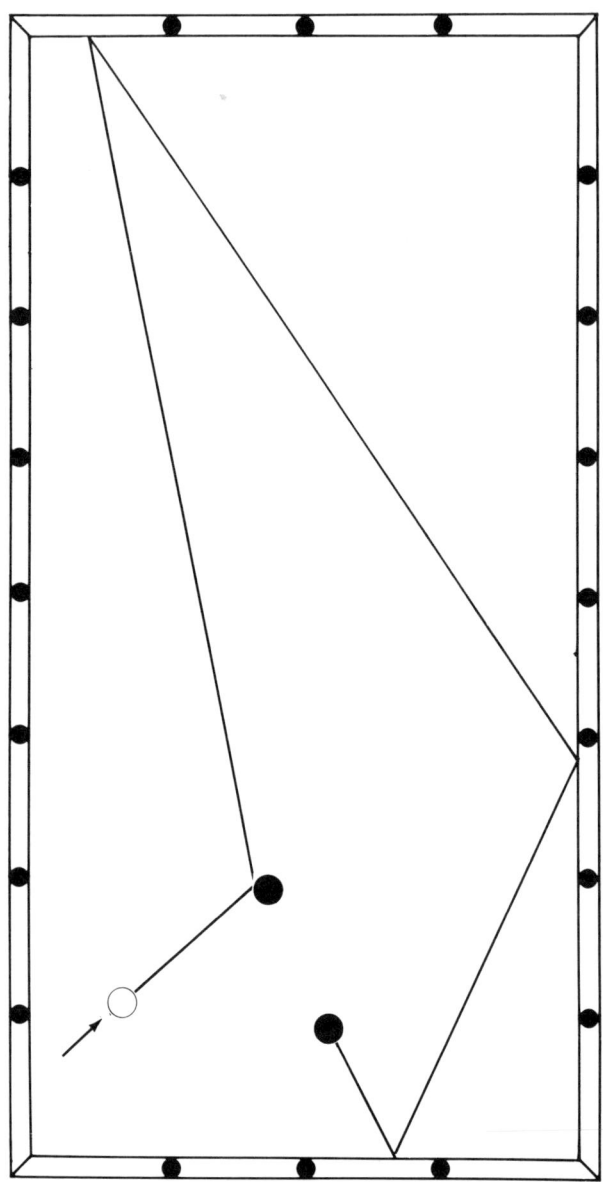

57. Here is a carom shot that is difficult because of the long trajectory the ball must travel. The key to a successful shot is learning to hit the correct spot on the first cushion. Use half a cue-tip width of draw on the cue ball.

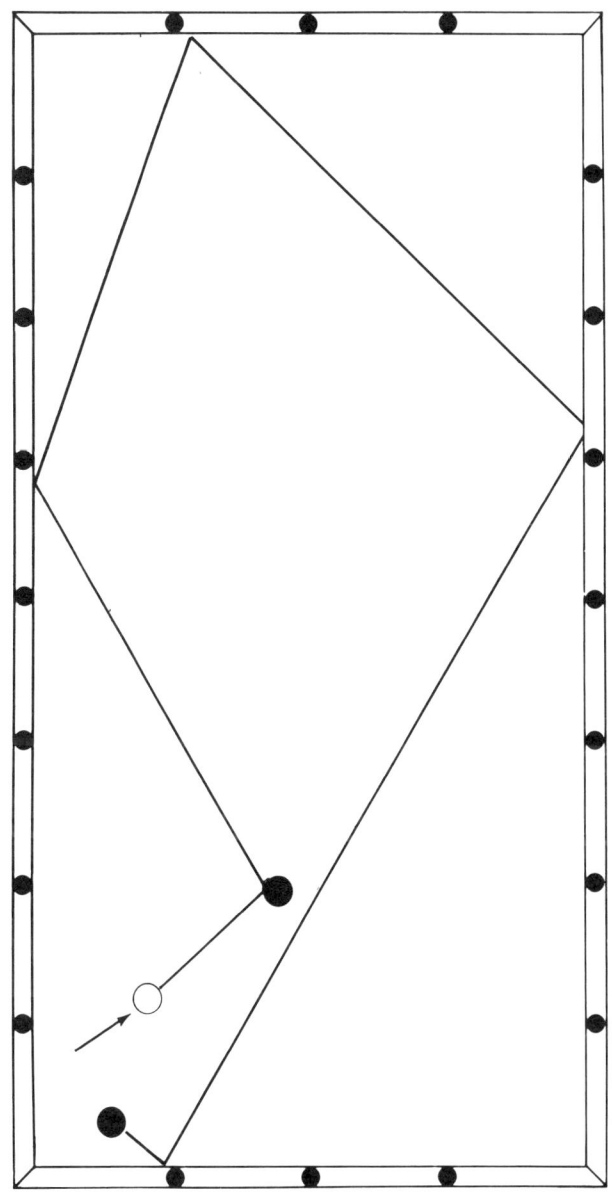

58. This interesting carom shot is a natural, and the shooter should use plenty of draw.

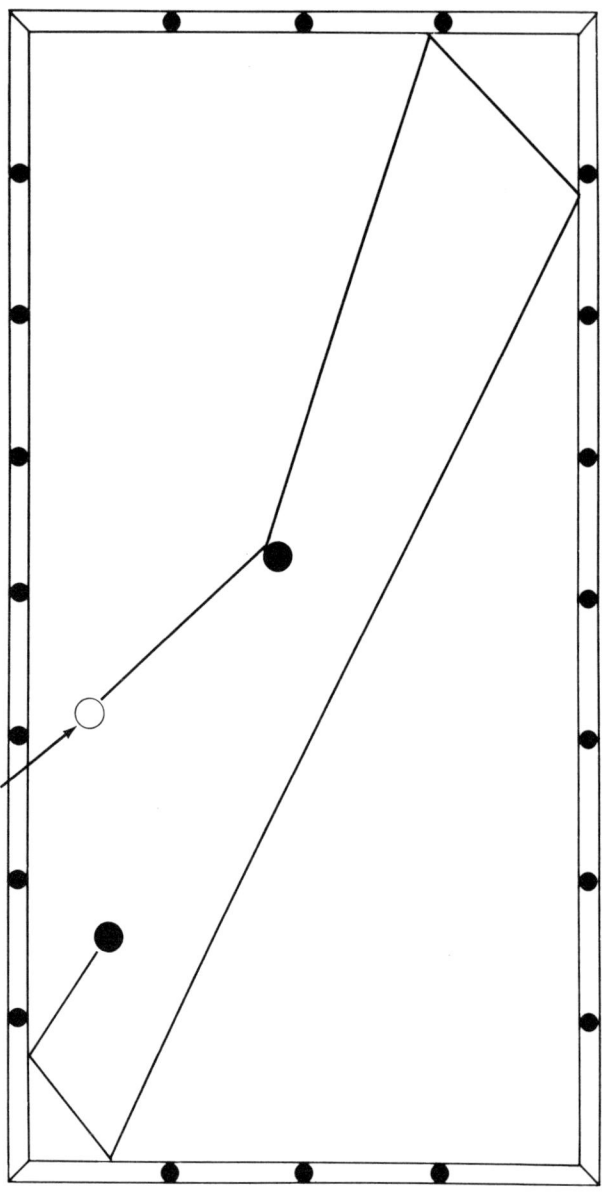

59. This carom shot to the top rail should not be too difficult and should build confidence in the beginning player.

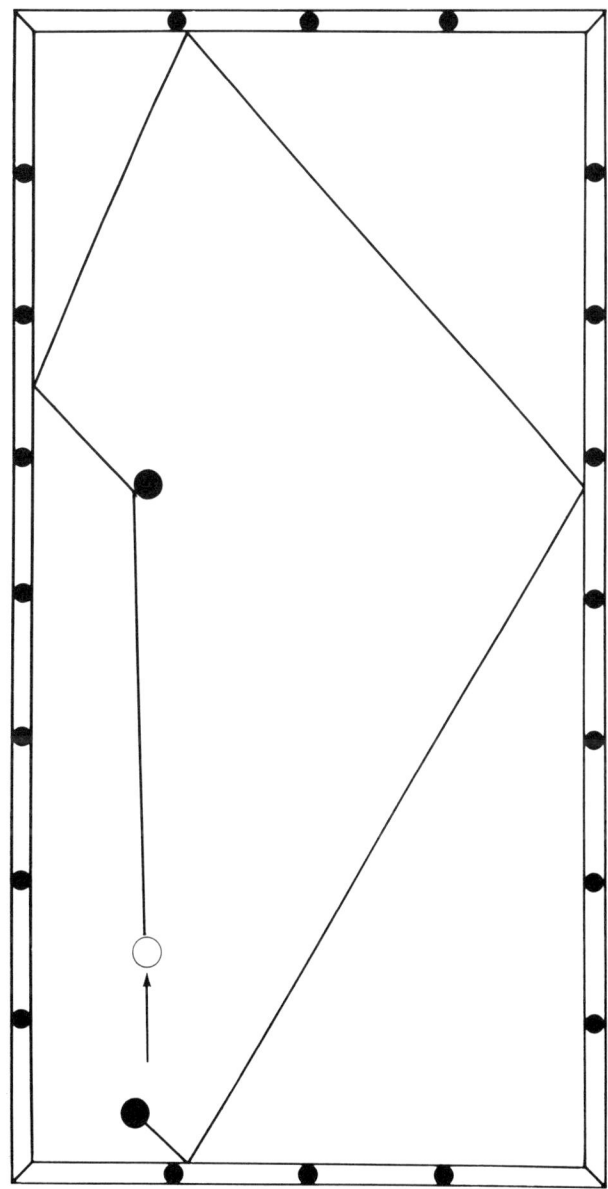

60. This carom shot is somewhat difficult because of the long trajectories involved, and, more importantly, a strong bridge is needed for accuracy when shooting over another ball.

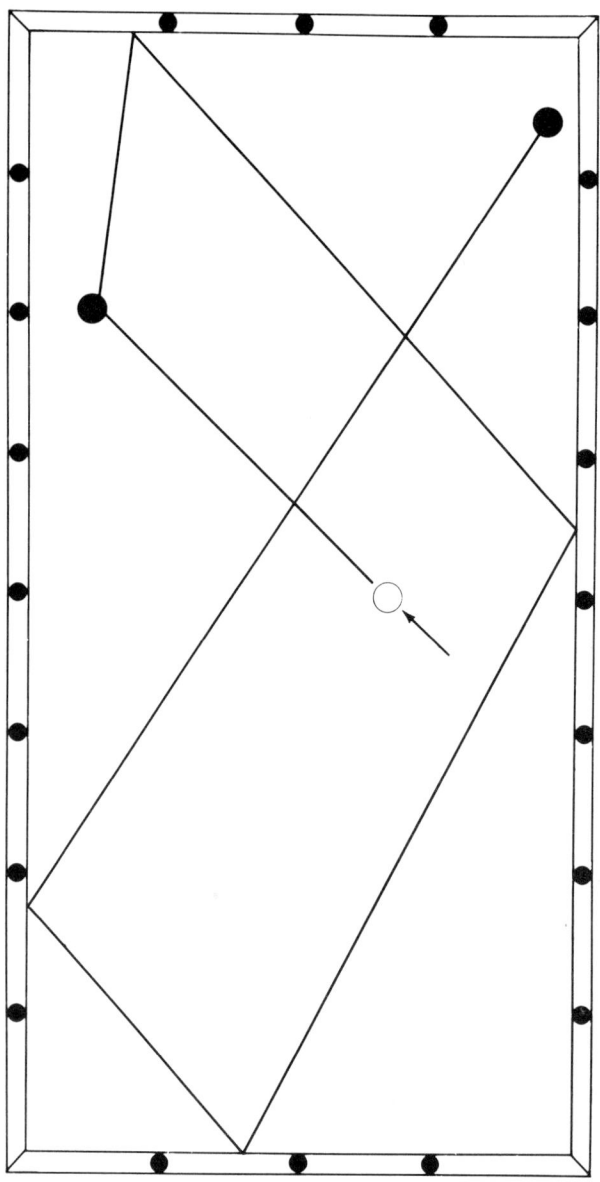

61. This shot, which caroms off the object ball and then strikes four cushions before reaching the second object ball, requires a strong stroke and a fair amount of draw on the cue ball.

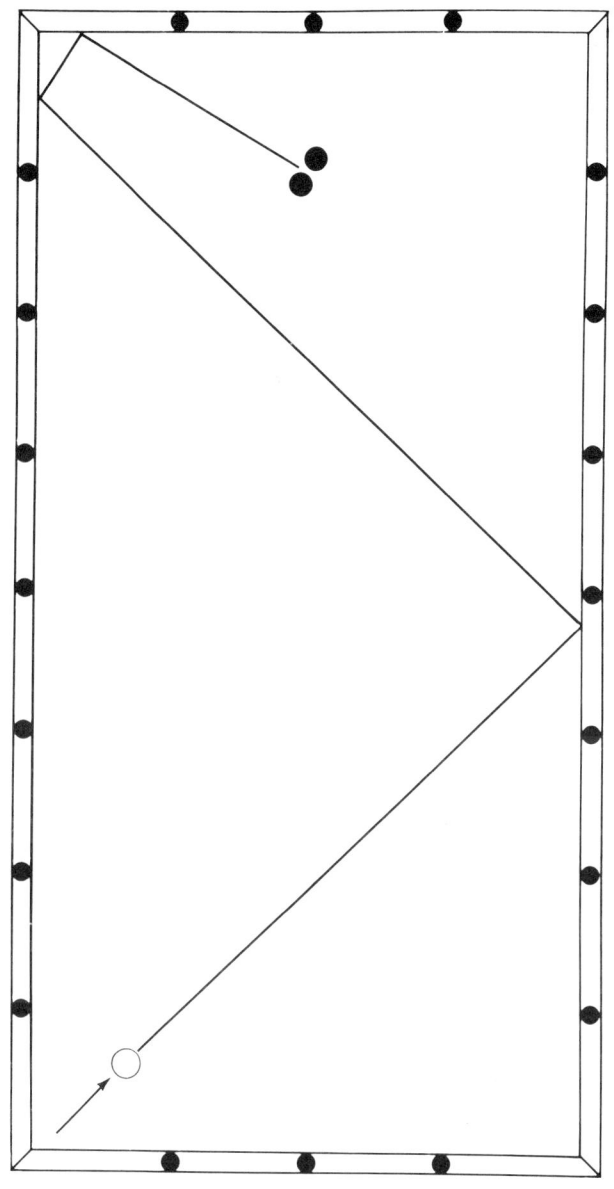

62. This is known as a reverse English bank shot.

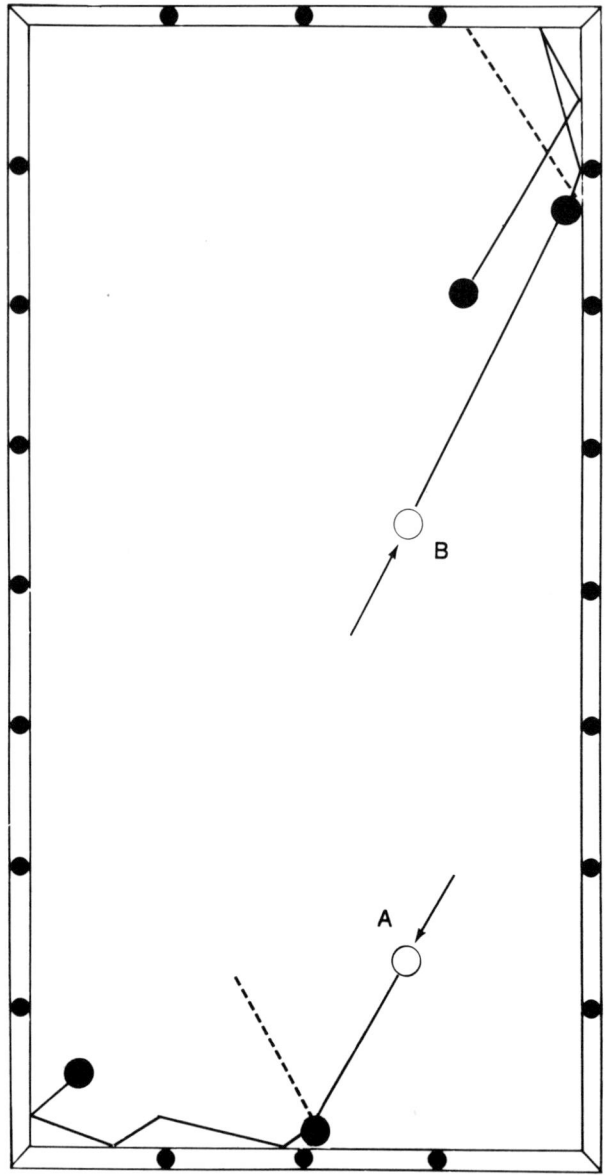

63. These two shots are known as force-follow shots. Basically they are double-rail shots in which the cue ball strikes the same rail more than once and then rebounds off its final cushion to strike the second object ball. *A* requires right English.

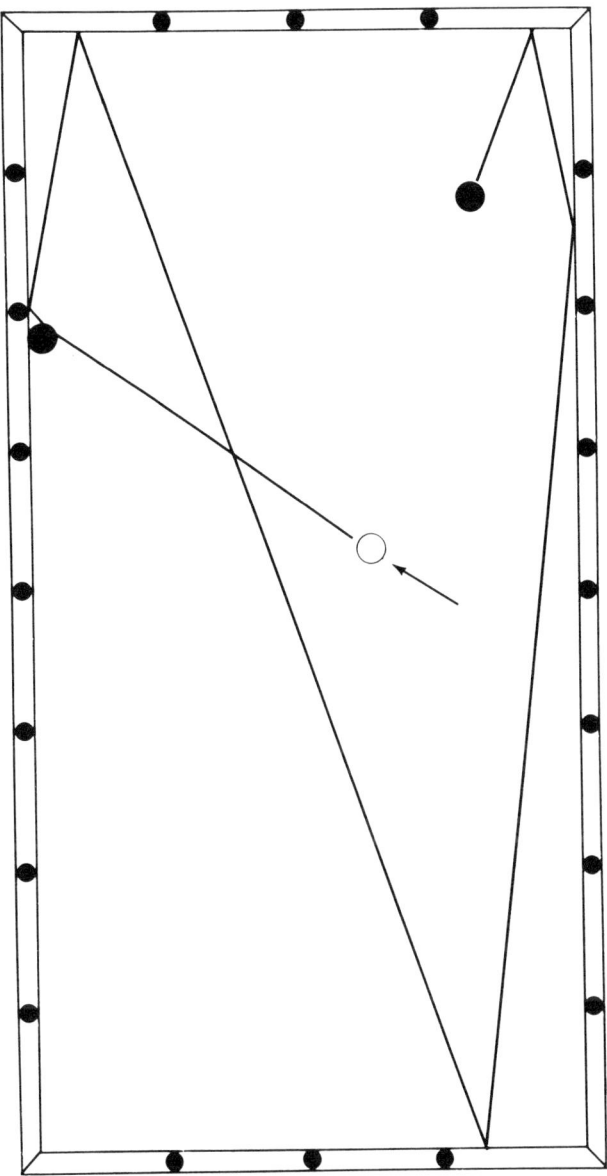

64. This five-cushion carom shot is known as a percentage shot and is well worth practicing. It is hit with a center-ball stroke or very slight right English.

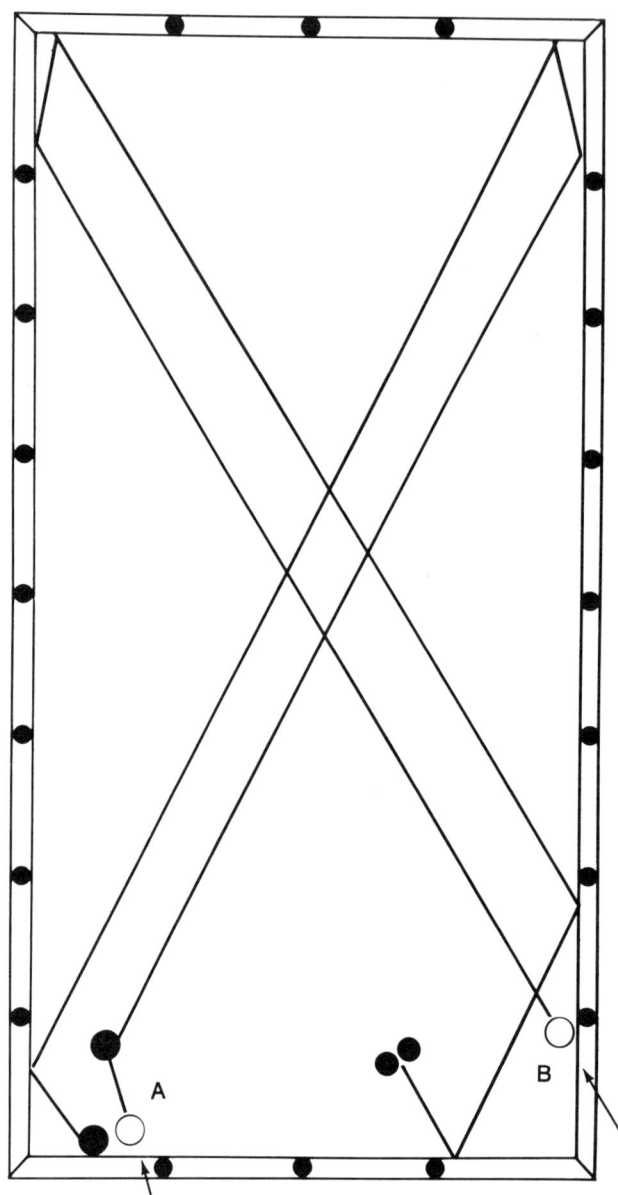

65. This diagram shows a center-ball carom shot *(A)* and a related reverse bank shot *(B)*. The carom shot involves properly cutting the first object ball and hence is more difficult.

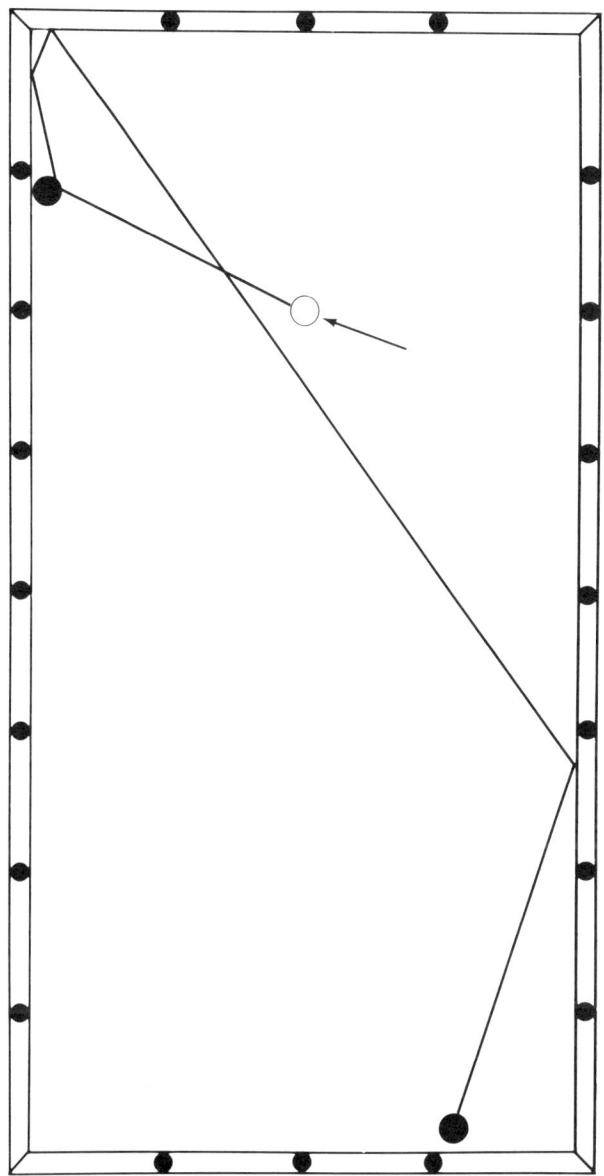

66. This unusual carom shot is known as a high-ball hit. Right English is used.

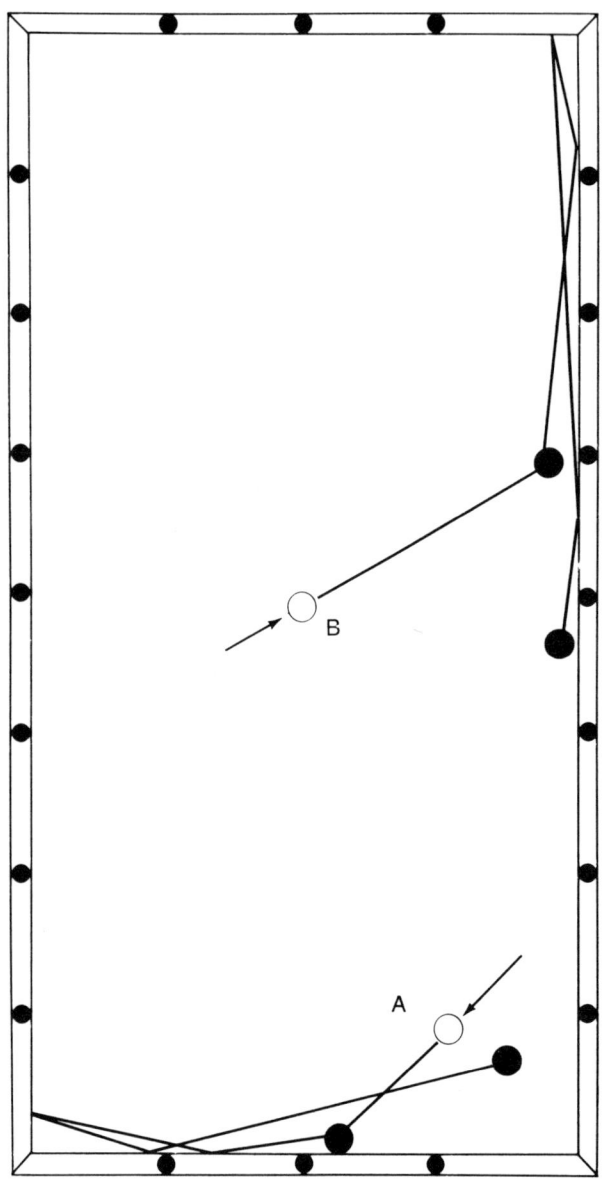

67. Here are two more examples of double-rail shots. *A* requires a center-ball stroke. In *B,* the cue ball is hit somewhat high and given some follow.

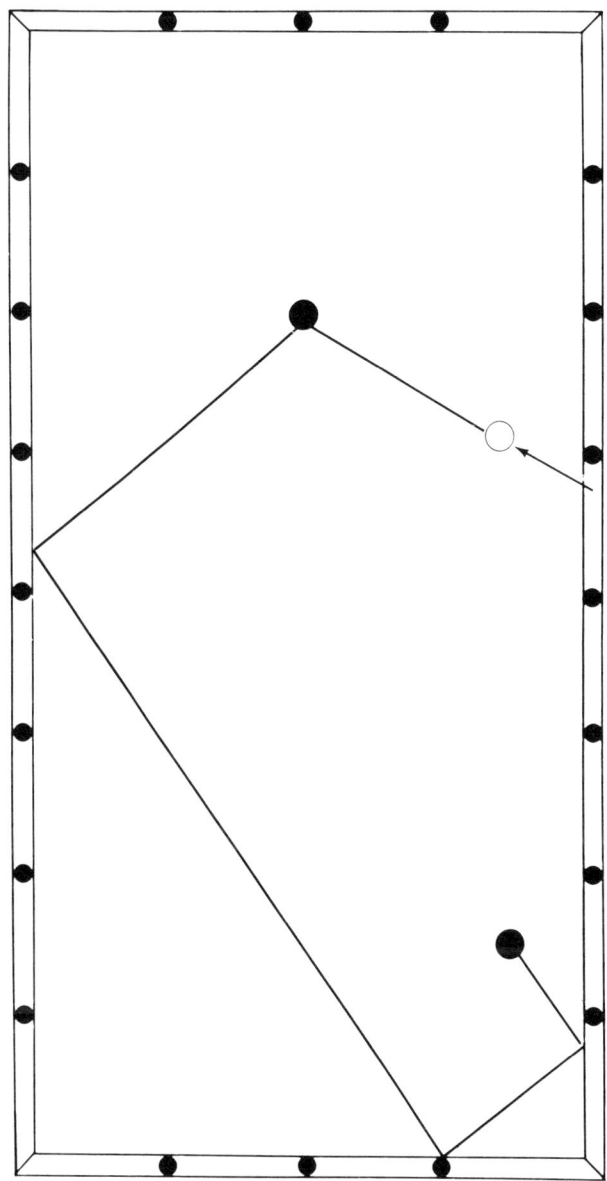

68. This carom shot requires heavy draw on the cue ball, and of course the trick is to apply heavy draw with enough force to enable the cue ball to complete its circuit around the table.

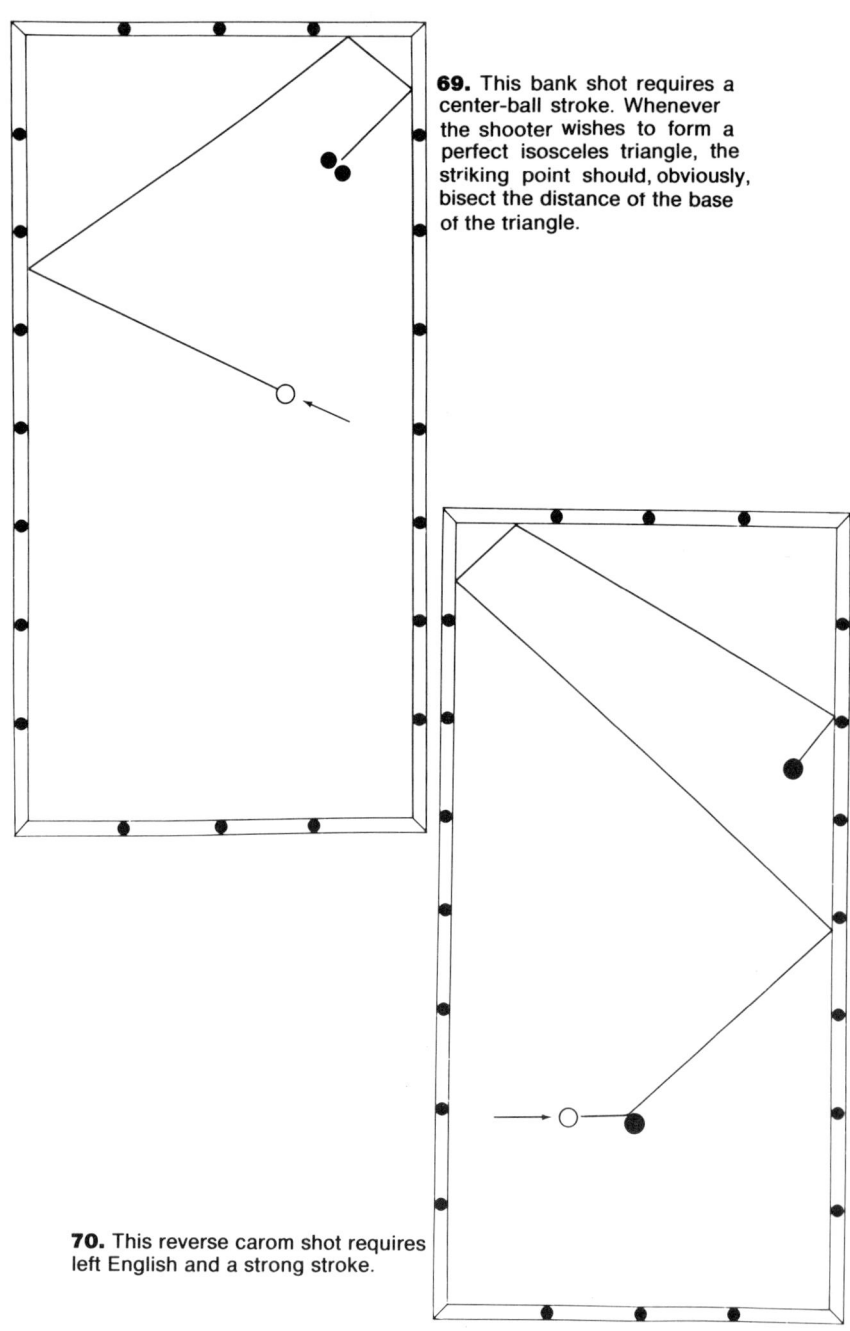

69. This bank shot requires a center-ball stroke. Whenever the shooter wishes to form a perfect isosceles triangle, the striking point should, obviously, bisect the distance of the base of the triangle.

70. This reverse carom shot requires left English and a strong stroke.

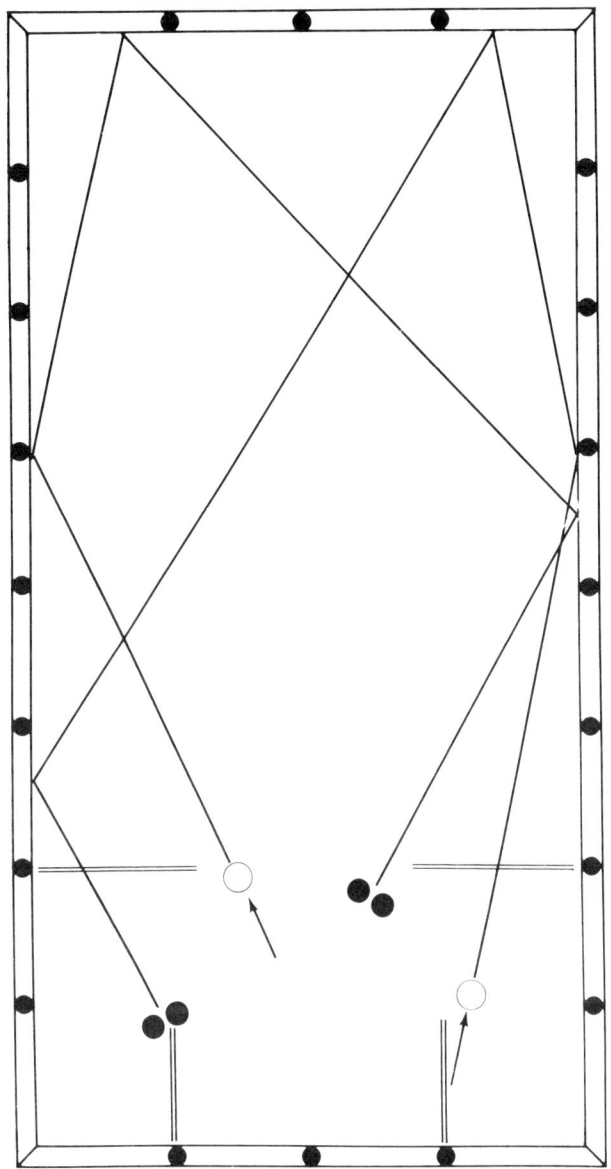

71. Here are two parallel bank shots. Note that the striking point is in each case the third diamond down, and that initially both cue ball and object balls were equidistant from the near end of the table and equidistant from the long rails.

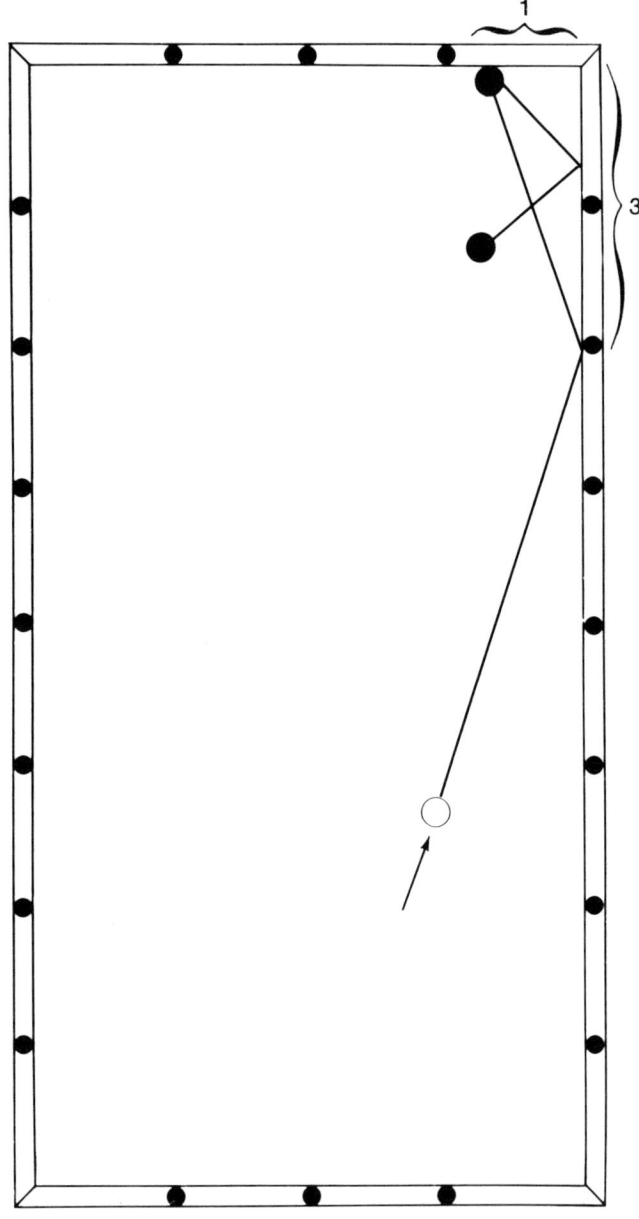

72. This is known as an S shot. To make it work, measure the distance of the first object ball from the near corner, and the striking point along the first cushion will be three times that distance down from the corner.

Review Notes

1. Be sure to select a cue that is right for you, one that is straight and feels properly balanced.
2. Make sure that the tip of your cue is neither too spongy nor too hard.
3. Whether actually at the table shooting, or even moving around it, you should be thoroughly relaxed.
4. Sight along the cue as you would along a gun, with your head directly over the line of aim.
5. A smooth, even stroke is essential in order to hit where you aim.
6. Seeing everything correctly is all-important. Step back from the table occasionally to get a better perspective.
7. Work hard on your form to develop a forceful stroke that can be made without too much effort. Develop a strong draw stroke.
8. No rules or systems can cover all situations, and constant practice and experience are essential. Develop the ability to adjust. Remember that the faster a ball is hit, the less will be the deflection caused by English, and the smaller will be the angle of rebound off the cushions.
9. For billiards, review the 5 system and the 2 system and the way in which diamonds are connected from the scoring point to the fourth cushion.

Glossary

Angle: The angle formed between the line of travel of the cue ball and the line of travel of the object ball, or the angle at which a ball rebounds from a cushion.

Balk Line: A line on the table which defines an area with restrictions on scoring.

Bank Shot: In pool, a shot in which the object ball is driven to one or more cushions before going into the pocket. In billiards, a shot in which the cue ball hits one or more cushions before striking an object ball.

Break: The opening shot of any game.

Called Ball: The object ball named by the shooter to be pocketed.

Call Shot: A requirement in Three-Cushion Caroms where players must designate every cushion hit before scoring.

Carom: A collision followed by a rebound, either when two balls strike each other, or when a ball strikes a cushion.

Count: A score or a point.

Cross-table: This term usually refers to shots scored by driving the cue ball across the table. Many three-cushion table shots are cross-table shots.

Cue Ball: The white ball hit by the cue stick.

Cue Ball in Hand: The player takes the cue ball in hand when, as a result of any error on the part of his opponent, he is allowed to put the ball in play at the point of his choice (within the rules).

Cushion or Rail: The covered resilient sides that border the playing surface of the table.

Diamonds: The spots inserted in the wooden rails used to help players judge angles.

Draw: A technique of hitting the cue ball below center with a firm, sharp grip, which causes the cue ball to return after striking the object ball.

English: The left or right twist or spin applied to the cue ball.

Fancy Shot: An exhibition shot requiring unusual skill; a trick shot.

Follow: Stroking above center on the cue ball so as to make it follow the course of the object ball after hitting it.

Follow-through: The movement of the shooter's arm after striking the cue ball.

Foot Spot: A spot equidistant from the center spot and the center diamond on the foot rail. It is used for spotting object balls.

Foul: Any violation of the rules; an unfair stroke.

Frozen: Two balls touching each other, or a ball touching a cushion.

Head Spot: A spot near the head of the table; the reverse of the foot spot.

Head String: A line drawn through the head spot connecting the diamonds on the long side rails near the head of the table.

High Run: The largest number of points scored in a single inning.

Inning: A turn at the table.

Lagging: A technique used by players to decide who breaks or shoots first. From a point below the foot spot, each player rebounds the cue ball off the far side of the table. The player whose cue ball rolls back closest to the foot rail decides who breaks.

Long String: Same as the Head String, but at the foot of the table.

Masse: Causing the cue ball to curve away from a straight line.

Miscue: A slip in stroking caused by improper handling of the cue.

Miss: A failure to do as intended.

Object Ball: Any ball other than the cue ball.

Penalties: The forfeiting of points for fouls.

Rack: A triangular frame in which fifteen balls are placed at the start of the game.

Reverse English: Causing the cue ball, after it hits a rail, to go in a direction other than the one indicated by the pointing of the cue. As opposed to natural English and center ball. (Many variations and definitions.)

Safety: A defensive measure taken in an effort to leave a very difficult shot for one's opponent.

Scratch: A shot after which a player gives up his turn at the table, usually by having one's cue ball go into a pocket unintentionally.

Set Up or **Hanger:** A simple shot—practically unmissable.

Spotting: Replacement of balls on the spots, usually after a scratch.

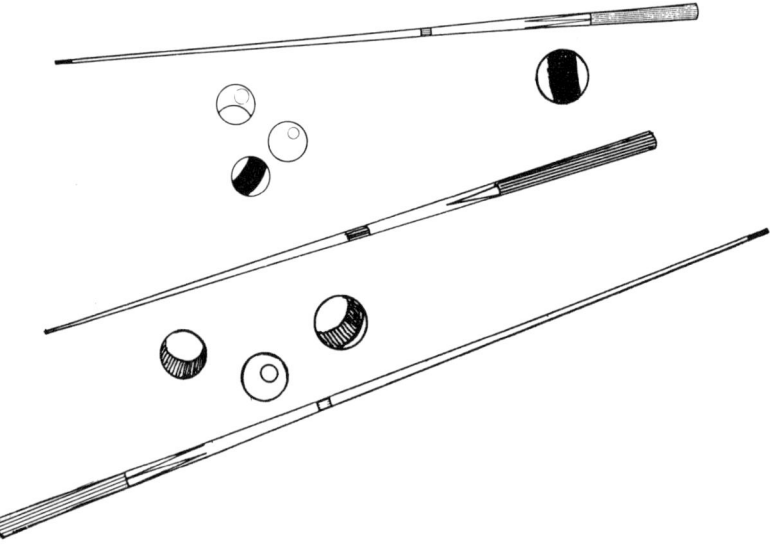

Index

Angle shot into a pocket corner
  oblique, 20
  simple, 19, 20

Balk-Line Billiards, 13
Balls, 8. *See also* Cue ball; Object balls
Bank-shot triangle, 30, 55
Bank shots
  five-cushion, 50
  four-cushion, 52
  parallel, 89
  proper English and, 64
  related reverse, 84
  requiring center-ball stroke, 88
  reverse English, 81
  seven-cushion, 51
Beginner's delight shots, 65
Break shots
  direct, 24
  one-cushion, 25
  requiring special bridge, 27
  three-cushion, 28
  two-cushion, 26
Bridge, the, 10
Byron, Lord, 7

Caesar, Julius, 6
Carom shots, 63
  center-ball, 74, 75, 84
  difficult, 62
  five-cushion, 83
  with heavy draw on cue ball, 87
  with long trajectory, 76
    using strong bridge, 79
  requiring strong stroke, 80
  reverse, using left English, 88
  to top rail, 78
  using plenty of draw, 77
  using right English, 85
Caroming into a combination shot, 43
Center-ball bank shots, four-cushion, 74
Center-ball carom shots, 74, 75, 84
Center-ball stroke, 69

China, 6–7
Cobb, Irwin, 7
Combination shots
  caroming into, 43
  simple, 33
  with two balls frozen together, 42
Cross-table shots, 32, 60
Cue ball
  altering position of, 70, 71
  controlling, 20, 21
  in the corner, difficult handling of, 66, 67, 68
  English and, 21
  five ways to hit, 12
  keeping in center of table, 34
  moving to opposite side of table, 39
  placing, 61
Cues, 8
Cut shots, long, 35

Direct break shots, 24
Double rail shots, 62, 82, 86
Draw stroke, 11–12

Eight Ball, 13, 15–16
England, 6–7
English
  cue ball and, 21
  left, using for reverse carom shots, 88
  light draw stroke and, 41
  proper, bank shots and, 64
  right
    carom shots using, 85
  use of, 12
Equipment, 8

Five-cushion bank shots, 50
Five-cushion carom shots, 83
5 system, 45–55
  basic principle of, 48
5-system shots from the 6 diamond on the short rail, 59
Follow stroke, 11–12

Follow-through, 11
Force-follow shots, 82
Four-cushion bank shots, 52
Four-cushion center-ball shots, 74
France, 6–7

Glossary, 92–94
Grip, 10

Hamilton, Alexander, 7
Henry, O., 7
High-ball hit, 75, 85
History of billiards and pool, 6–7
Hoppe, Willie, 7

Isosceles triangle, making a perfect, 55
Italy, 6–7
Ivory balls, 8

Jefferson, Thomas, 7
Jonson, Ben, 7

Lafayette, Marquis de, 7
Light draw strokes, right English and, 41
Lincoln, Abraham, 7
London, Jack, 7
Long cut shots, 35
Louis XIV, King, 7

Mary, Queen of Scots, 7
Mosconi, Willie, 10

Nero, Emperor, 6
Nine Ball, 13, 16

Object balls
  aiming and hitting, 11
  caroming off, 61
  against cushion, 29
  cutting, 31
  frozen on the rail, 37
  hitting at different points, 21
  range of positions for, 70, 71
One-cushion break shots, 25
One-cushion shots, tricky, 36
One Pocket, 13, 17

Parallel bank shots, 89
Parallels, principle of, 53, 54
Percentage shots, 83
Phelan, Michael, 7
Plastic balls, 8

Pocket billiards, 4, 5
  equipment for, 8
Position play, 13
  mastering, 22

Rail shots, double, 62, 82, 86
Red Ball Billiards, 13
Related reverse bank shots, 84
Reverse carom shots, using left English, 88
Reverse English bank shots, 81
Review notes, 91
Roosevelt, Theodore, 7
Rotation, 13, 15
Runyon, Damon, 7

S shots, 90
Secreiter, John, 7
Seven-cushion bank shots, 51
Shakespeare, William, 7
Shot when behind rack of balls, 23
Six balls exercise, 40
Slosson's Billiard Room, 7
Spain, 6–7
Stance, 9–10
Straight Billiards, 13
Straight Pool, 13, 14–15
Striking long rail first, 69, 70
Stroke, 11
  draw, 11–12
  follow, 11–12

Tables, 8
Three-cushion break shots, 28
Three-Cushion Caroms, 4, 5, 13, 44–45
  equipment for, 8
Three-Cushion Caroms Tournament, 4
Three-cushion shots, 38
Trajectories, bringing closer together, 72, 73
Triangle, isosceles, making a perfect, 55
Twain, Mark, 7
Two-cushion break shots, 26
2 (or 2-plus) system, 56–58

Umbrella shots, 69

Vignaux, Maurice, 7

Washington, George, 7
World's Balk-Line Championship (1906), 7